# ⟶ BAKE

Would you like to learn to be a better baker?

We know that so many people watch *The Great British Bake Off* for the tips and techniques you pick up – not only from the judges, but from watching the bakers too. We wanted to distil that knowledge into a library of cookbooks that are specifically designed to take you from novice to expert baker. Individually, each book covers the skills you will want to perfect so that you can master a particular area of baking – everything from cakes to bread, sweet pastries to pies.

We have chosen recipes that are classics of each type, and grouped them together so that they take you on a progression from 'Easy does it' through 'Needs a little skill' to 'Up for a challenge'. Put together, the full series of books will give you a comprehensive collection of the best recipes, along with all the advice you need to become a better baker.

The triumphs and lessons of the bakers in the tent show us that not everything works every time. But I hope that with these books as your guide, we have given you a head start towards baking it better every time!

—

*Linda Collister*
Series Editor

## – BAKE IT BETTER –

# BISCUITS

*Annie Rigg*

HODDER &
STOUGHTON

# Contents

## BAKE IT BETTER
*Baker's Guide*

## BAKE IT BETTER
*Recipes*

*Easy does it*    38

## Need a little skill 88

## Up for a challenge 134

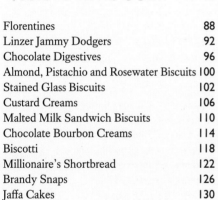

# Welcome bakers!

There are few greater pleasures than sitting down with a cup of tea and a home-made biscuit – and this book offers 40 classic biscuit recipes to get you going.

As well as being great bakes, the recipes have been carefully chosen to introduce you to all the key techniques, like rubbing-in, creaming, shaping and piping, that not only set you up to bake better biscuits, but which you can use in all sorts of other bakes.

Start with the 'Easy does it' section and master the basics with recipes like Icebox Cookies, then, as you grow in confidence, you can be ready to move to the recipes that 'Need a little skill' – Linzer Jammy Dodgers perhaps, some delectable Viennese Whirls. And the more you bake, the sooner you will find that you are 'Up for a challenge' with sophisticated Mochaccino Macarons, or testing your decorating skills with a stunning fairy tale Gingerbread House.

The colour strip on the right-hand side of the page tells you at a glance the level of difficulty of the recipe (from one spoon for easy to three spoons for more of a challenge), and gives you a helpful checklist of the special equipment you will use. Before you begin, have a look at the Baker's Guide at the beginning of the book. That will tell you what equipment you need to get started (just a bowl, a spoon and a baking tray will do!), introduce you to the most important ingredients, and explain some terms and techniques in more detail.

Biscuits can be a simple snack or a comforting mouthful of love, but even the most basic biscuit is a joy to make and eat. The *Bake It Better: Biscuits* book will show you just what you can do with butter, sugar, flour and eggs, so let's grab our wooden spoons and get baking!

## HOW TO USE THIS BOOK

### SECTION 1: BAKER'S GUIDE
Read this section before you start baking. The Baker's Guide contains key information on ingredients (page 10), equipment (page 16) and skills (page 22) relevant to the recipes in the book.

Refer back the Baker's Guide when you're baking if you want a refresher on a particular skill. In the recipes the first mention of each skill is highlighted in bold.

### SECTION 2: RECIPES
Colour strips on the right-hand side and 1, 2 or 3 spoons show the level of difficulty of the recipe. Within the colour strips you'll find helpful information to help you decide what to bake: Hands-on time; Baking time; Quantity and Special equipment.

Refresh your knowledge of any Essential skills by referring to the Baker's Guide before you get started.

Refer back to the Baker's Guide when a skill is highlighted in bold in the recipe if you need a reminder.

Try Something Different options are given where the recipe lends itself to experimenting with ingredients or decorations.

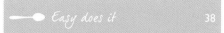

# BAKE IT BETTER

# Baker's Guide

# Ingredients

The simplest biscuits require just a few ingredients: butter, sugar, flour and maybe an egg, but usually you'll be adding flavourings to these key elements. Knowing a bit more about the ingredients before you use them will help to avoid problems and lead to more successful bakes. Here are a few simple guidelines to bear in mind when you're buying, storing and using your ingredients.

## BAKING POWDER, BICARBONATE OF SODA AND CREAM OF TARTAR

Baking powder and bicarbonate of soda are chemical raising agents commonly used in baking, most often in small quantities, to lighten the texture of biscuits as well as to create volume and produce a tender crumb. Baking powder is a blend of bicarbonate of soda (an alkali) and cream of tartar (an acid) and sometimes also corn or rice flour to absorb any moisture that might be present. The two raising agents work by reacting with the moisture in your biscuit, and the heat from the oven, to produce carbon dioxide bubbles that lift, and lighten, the crumb.

Baking powder and bicarbonate of soda are not interchangeable and make sure you use exactly the amount stated. Check the best before date on the packets too, and discard any out-of-date or damp raising agents, as they lose their potency when they get past their best and they won't give you a good bake.

If you've run out of baking powder when you come to bake, you can make your own. For 1 teaspoon of baking powder, simply combine half a teaspoon cream of tartar with a quarter teaspoon of bicarbonate of soda.

## BUTTER

In this book the recipes generally use **unsalted butter**, as it has a mild, delicate flavour, gives a lovely golden colour to your bakes and allows the baker to add salt to taste, if they wish. Unsalted butter usually contains slightly less whey than **salted butter** and it's this that bakers believe gives a more evenly coloured bake. Salted butter can also be used, but it may have a stronger taste. If you do use salted butter in a sweet recipe you won't need to add any extra salt.

Instructions are given in each recipe for whether your butter should be used at room temperature, softened or chilled. For recipes that require you to cream the mixture, use the butter at room temperature so that it's easier to smoothly incorporate dry ingredients, such as sugar; chilled and diced butter is needed for recipes that start by rubbing butter into dry ingredients, such as flour. To keep your butter at its best, store it tightly wrapped in its original wrapper in the fridge away from strong flavours, or you can freeze it, wrapped, for up to a month.

## CHOCOLATE

Try to use the best-quality chocolate that you can find, as it can really affect the flavour of your final bake. Good chocolate is now widely available in supermarkets and you can buy chips in larger bags from specialist suppliers online.

Store bars of chocolate well wrapped in a cool, dry, dark cupboard, and away from other strong-tasting or flavoured ingredients. Always make sure that you've chopped your chocolate before melting it, to ensure that it melts quickly and evenly without scorching (see page 31 for more melting tips).

**Dark chocolate** with around 70 per cent cocoa solids is the type used in most of the recipes in this book as it gives the best flavour – chocolate with a higher percentage of cocoa (75 per cent and above) may be too bitter for general tastes, while a lower percentage may be too sweet.

**Milk chocolate** has a milder, sweeter flavour than dark, but the same rules apply and you should always use one that has the highest percentage of cocoa solids you can find, not only for better flavour but because the chocolate will set slightly firmer.

**White chocolate** doesn't contain any cocoa solids, just cocoa butter, and can vary a lot in quality, with some children's bars containing hardly any cocoa butter at all. Ideally, look for something with 30 per cent cocoa butter or more, but be aware that the higher fat content in white chocolate means that it will set less firmly than dark or milk chocolates.

COCOA POWDER

A dark, unsweetened powder made from pure cocoa with nearly all the cocoa butter removed – it is very bitter and strongly flavoured, and will give a powerful chocolate hit to your baking. Cocoa powder shouldn't be confused for, or substituted with, drinking chocolate, which has had sugar and dried milk powder added to it.

DRIED FRUIT

Keep stores of dried fruit such as raisins, sultanas and currants out of direct sunlight and in sealed containers for freshness, but bear in mind that dried fruit is best bought as and when you need it. Candied peel is widely available ready chopped, but can also be found in boxes as whole pieces of orange, lemon or citrus peel, allowing you to cut the pieces into a size and mix that you prefer.

EGGS

Eggs bind your mixtures together, providing richness and lightening batters by incorporating air, particularly in recipes like Sponge Fingers (see page 70). All the recipes in this book use medium-sized eggs (about 62–65g each) – using a different-sized egg from the one specified can affect your recipe by altering the texture and moisture of the dough.

Storing eggs in the fridge, pointed-side down, protects the yolk from drying out and spoiling. Keep them in the box they came in and in the cooler body of the fridge, not the door, and use by the best before date on the box. If a recipe calls for only egg yolks, you can keep the spare egg whites, covered, in the fridge for 3–4 days, or they will freeze well for up to a month: defrost thoroughly before use. (A good tip is to mark the quantity on the container before you put it in the freezer.)

Eggs should be used at room temperature as they give a greater volume when beaten, so bring them out of the fridge 30–60 minutes before you need to use them.

EXTRACTS AND FLAVOURINGS

Avoid the synthetic versions of flavourings wherever possible, as these can give your bake a rather unpleasant 'fake' taste.

**Vanilla extract** is now widely available. Try to avoid the cheaper vanilla flavouring or essence on offer, which is a chemical, rather than natural flavouring. Check the label for 'natural' or 'pure' vanilla extract, which means it's been extracted from the vanilla pods and so you will only need to use a small amount. Whole **vanilla pods** are a good addition to your store cupboard, and once used you can dry them off and pop them into a jar of caster sugar. They will lightly infuse the sugar with their flavour and it can be used in biscuit recipes. Jars of highly concentrated **vanilla bean paste** are another good addition for the store cupboard, and are slightly less expensive than vanilla pods.

**Coffee** flavour can be added to recipes by using instant espresso powder or granules dissolved in a little boiling water. It adds a lovely strong coffee flavour to icings. You can also use coffee essence, although some find the flavour a little strange.

**Ground spices** should be measured carefully and kept in screw-topped jars rather than open packs. Try to use them when they are still fresh, preferably within a few months of opening.

**Stem ginger** in syrup is a wonderful store cupboard ingredient that adds an extra pop of gingery-ness to Gingersnaps (page 62). Drain the chunks of their syrup before using.

## FLOUR

Poor-quality or past-its-best flour can really affect the final taste and texture of your bake, so only use flour when it's fresh and store it correctly between uses: keep opened packs of flour either in tightly sealed storage jars, plastic food boxes or plastic food bags to stop it getting damp. Don't add new flour to old in storage jars, and aim to use it within a month of opening or by its best before date.

**Wheat flours** are the most commonly used flours in baking. Most recipes call for **plain flour**, which needs sifting to give lightness to your biscuits. **Spelt flour** adds a slight nutty taste and a more crumbly texture; it can be substituted in part for plain flour, but isn't really suitable for delicate biscuit work. **Wholemeal flour** is good for recipes that require a more oaty, wholesome flavour and texture and, along with oatmeal, is a key ingredient in Chocolate Digestives and Oatmeal Biscuits for Cheese (pages 96 and 58). **Rice flour**, used in small quantities, gives an almost gritty texture to your bake, while **cornflour** can be added to Shortbread and Viennese Whirls (pages 54 and 78) to give a delicate crumb.

**Gluten-free flours** are wheat-free mixtures made from several ingredients, including rice, potato, tapioca, maize, chickpea, broad bean, white sorghum or buckwheat, and are readily and inexpensively available. Ready-mixed gluten-free flours sometime suggest adding xanthum gum (which comes in powder form) to help improve the texture and crumb of your bake – check the packet and if your mix doesn't include it add 1 teaspoon xanthum gum per 150g flour. Some flours may also require a little more liquid to make the dough manageable. Gluten-free flours vary in taste and texture from brand to brand, so it's worth trying a few out to see which you prefer.

## HONEY

Look out for honey that comes from the nectar of a single variety of flower or plant (such as orange blossom), as the flavour should be more distinct. As a general rule, the paler the honey, the milder the flavour. You can use almost any type in baking, although soft-set honey (but not honeycomb) is the easiest to blend in. If you don't have any, solid honey can be softened first by gently warming it in the microwave, or in a dish set in a bowl of warm water.

## ICING SUGAR

This fine, powdered white sugar dissolves easily in icings and buttercream, but also gives the light, melt-in-the-mouth texture to Viennese Whirls (page 78), and is used to dust finished biscuits. Sift it well to remove any lumps before use.

**Royal icing sugar** is a mixture of icing sugar and dried egg white that can be mixed with water to make a stiff white icing or a decorative 'glue' for recipes such as the Gingerbread House (page 154) – just add water, bit by bit, and beat well until the desired consistency is achieved.

**Unrefined golden icing sugar** has a slight butterscotch flavour and can be substituted for regular icing sugar in both biscuit doughs and icings, but you won't get the brilliant white colour you get from white icing sugar.

## JAMS AND SPREADS

Perfect for sandwiching or filling biscuits, and for adding a splash of colour to your bakes. It's also useful to keep a jar of chocolate and hazelnut spread, or a caramel sauce like dulce de leche, in your cupboard, as both make utterly delicious quick cookie or macaron fillings.

## MARGARINES AND SPREADS

These are based on vegetable oils, with added salt and flavourings. Some are made specifically for baking and can be used straight from the fridge; they give good results but they won't taste quite the same as bakes made with butter.

Spreads designed for use on breads and crackers are not meant for baking and won't give a good bake as they contain too much water and not enough fat.

**Dairy-free spreads** can be substituted for butter in recipes that require softened, or room-temperature, butter. These spreads are usually made from a blend of vegetable and sunflower oils and can be used straight from the fridge, although they may lack a little of the richness of pure butter.

## NUTS AND SEEDS

It's best to buy nuts and seeds in small quantities as they can become oily and rancid when past their best, especially **walnuts** and **pine nuts**. Store them in a screwtop jar, or airtight container in a cool, dark spot and use them before their best before date.

**Almonds** are particularly versatile in baking and can be used whole, blanched and flaked or ground.

**Blanched hazelnuts** have had their thin, papery brown skin removed, but this is easy enough to do if you only have unblanched – just tip the nuts onto a baking sheet and toast them in a medium oven for 4–5 minutes. Gather the toasted nuts into a clean tea towel and rub them vigorously to remove the skins.

Look out for packs of **mixed seeds** (usually a combination of sunflower, pumpkin, sesame and linseed) to add to flapjacks and oatmeal cookies. Toasting nuts increases their flavour, but they do burn easily, so watch them carefully.

## OILS

Some recipes for softer, chewier biscuits require **sunflower oil** or **groundnut oil**, both of which have a mild, neutral flavour and should not be confused with **vegetable oil**, a frying oil which will give a distinctive, unpleasant 'savoury' flavour to your baking.

Coconut oil is now widely available from health food shops and larger supermarkets and can be substituted for butter or to make recipes dairy-free. It often comes in jars and you'll need to gently melt it, either in the microwave, or in a pan, over a low heat, before using.

## SUGAR

There are various ways to sweeten biscuits, but it is very important to use the type of sugar specified in the recipe. They all combine with other ingredients in slightly different ways and this affects the end result.

**Caster sugar** is the refined white version. It has a mild, neutral sweetness and is easily combined with other ingredients.

**Golden caster sugar** is unrefined and gives a warmer, richer flavour, but it is not so easily combined, so techniques such as creaming will take slightly longer.

**Soft light brown sugar**, **demerara sugar** or **light muscovado sugar** are all good when a warmer butterscotch or caramel flavour is needed and add a good, rich colour to biscuits. All these sugars should be stored in airtight bags or jars to stop them drying out, but if lumps do form, just press them out through a sieve.

## SYRUPS AND TREACLE

Syrups and treacles are perfect for adding sweetness and flavour to fillings and icings. **Golden syrup** and sticky **black treacle** will give your bakes a rich, rounded and warm toffee-ish flavour.

Treacle can be awkward and messy to measure and weigh, but if you sit the whole tin in a bowl of just-boiled water, or warm the measuring spoon in a mug of boiled water beforehand, you will find it much easier and less messy by far.

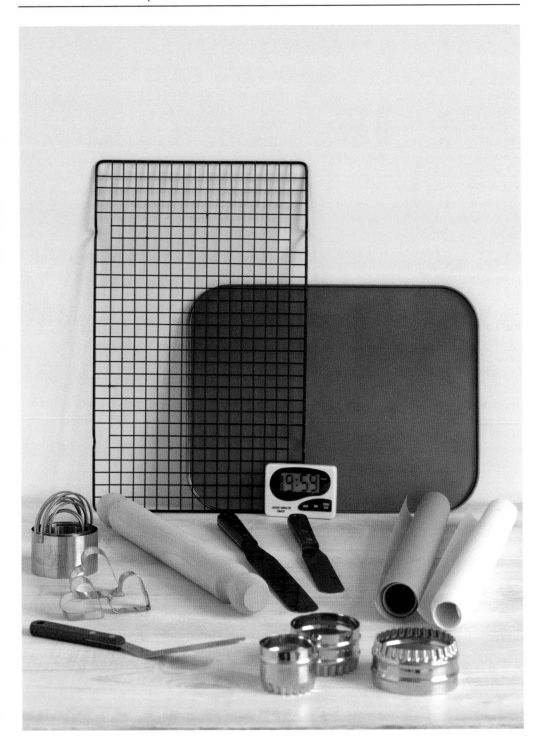

# Equipment

One of the best things about baking biscuits is that you can get started without a cupboard full of expensive equipment. In fact, you can probably produce your first tray of delicious biscuits with what you already have in your kitchen. But having a few key pieces of kit will make your life easier and more importantly will ensure your bakes are more consistently successful.

## BAKING PAPER AND SILICONE BAKING MATS

**Non-stick baking paper**, **parchment paper** and **silicone baking mats** are all non-stick liners and are invaluable for stopping biscuits sticking to trays and sheets. Silicone baking mats are expensive but they are reusable and if looked after properly they will last a long time. **Greaseproof paper** is best kept for wrapping cooked biscuits as it is water resistant, but its waxy coating doesn't stand up well to the heat of the oven. It is also not non-stick, so you will end up wrestling your biscuits off the paper after baking.

## BAKING SHEETS AND TRAYS

Sturdy sheets and trays that won't buckle and twist in the oven ensure your biscuits bake evenly. **Baking sheets** with only one raised edge make it easy to slide a palette knife under very thin biscuits. For other types of biscuits, a **baking tray** with sides is perfectly fine, just so long as you can easily get 10–12 biscuits per tray. It's worth having two or three baking sheets so that you can portion out and prepare a whole recipe's worth of dough at once, without having to wait for your sheets to cool down between batches.

## BISCUIT CUTTERS

A nest of cutters in various sizes is ideal – double-sided ones (plain and fluted) mean you won't need to buy two separate sets. Metal cutters will give you the cleanest edge when cutting out your biscuits. There's a cutter shape for just about any occasion or theme, as well as cutters for specific biscuits, such as bourbons or custard creams, and kits for embossing lettering into dough.

## BOWLS

If you're buying new, a nest of small, medium and large bowls is ideal. **Heatproof glass** bowls are perfect for sitting over a pan of simmering water and for putting in the microwave. **Stainless steel** are also good, but not microwave-proof. **Ceramic** bowls are pretty, can go in the dishwasher and are good for mixing by hand as they are less likely to slide all over the work surface, but they're quite heavy and break easily. **Plastic** bowls are cheap and good for weighing ingredients – some even have rubber bases, helping to make them non-slip. (You can solve the slip issue by placing a damp cloth underneath any bowl.) **Anodised aluminium** bowls are very durable and will last a lifetime, but, gaian, are no good in the microwave.

## COOLING RACKS

Wire cooling racks allow the air to circulate underneath your bakes, helping prevent the dreaded soggy bottom. For biscuits, look out for large rectangular cooling racks that will hold at least 24 biscuits in rows. If you need to, you can always improvise by using clean wire grill-pan racks for bigger biscuits, but smaller bakes are better on the finer wires of a cooling rack.

## FOOD-PROCESSOR OR MINI WHIZZER

Like a free-standing electric mixer, a food-processor is not essential, but it certainly makes light work of tasks like rubbing butter into flour (see page 23), or finely chopping nuts. If space is at a premium, a mini whizzer or chopper (a mini food-processor that chops about 100g of ingredients) is useful – they're good for small quantities and can be stored away quite easily when not in use.

## ICE CREAM SCOOP

Not essential, but a really useful piece of equipment for scooping out balls of biscuit dough in recipes that don't require rolling and stamping out.

## KNIVES

You'll probably find that a **medium-sized sharp knife** is useful for most purposes. When choosing a knife, hold it first to check that it feels well balanced, and that the weight and shape suits the size of your hand – a 20cm knife is probably the most versatile, but choose the one that you feel most comfortable with. If you can, spend a bit more on a good-quality knife; it will be worth every penny as it will be sturdier and last longer, and will be easier to keep sharp (a **knife sharpener** is vital too) for those really clean lines when trimming rolled-out dough and slicing up logs of biscuit dough.

Knives are made from different materials. The main ones to consider are stainless steel, which is cheaper but needs to be sharpened regularly; carbon steel, which is more expensive, harder and easier to keep sharp; and ceramic, which is far harder than carbon steel, much lighter and doesn't require sharpening – but can chip easily.

## LARGE METAL SPOON

A large, long-handled metal spoon for folding wet ingredients into dry is invaluable.

## MEASURING JUGS

Pick a heat-resistant and microwave-safe jug that's easy to read in both metric and imperial measures, starting from 50ml, if you can find one, otherwise 100ml and going up to about 2 litres. A small jug or cup that measures from 1 teaspoon (5ml) up to 4 tablespoons (60ml) is a useful extra, but remember you can also weigh liquids, as well as measuring the volume: 1ml = 1 gram. This is the most precise method.

## MEASURING SPOONS

Most measuring spoons come in sets of 4–6 different sizes, from ⅛ teaspoon to 1½ tablespoon, and are essential for ensuring absolute accuracy, especially when adding spices or raising agents. Day-to-day teaspoons, dessertspoons and tablespoons can vary enormously in size and will give inconsistent results to your bakes, so do invest in some proper measuring spoons. Look out, too, for measuring spoons with narrow pointed ends that will easily fit into small spice jars. Unless otherwise indicated, all spoon measures in these recipes are level – knock off the excess using a finger or the back of a knife.

## OVEN THERMOMETER

We all know how varied ovens can be, with some getting hotter than they should and some not getting hot enough; to be really accurate it's a good idea to get an oven thermometer. You can then check that your oven is reaching the correct temperature – and you can discover where the hot and cooler spots are – so your bakes cook evenly and perfectly.

## PALETTE KNIVES

An essential piece of kit for biscuit baking, **palette knives** are useful for spreading mixtures in tins, smoothing icing and for lifting biscuits from baking sheets. A small **offset palette knife**, with a kink in the frame, is perfect for spreading buttercream onto your biscuits or fillings when sandwiching them together.

## PASTRY BRUSH

This is an indispensable tool, particularly useful when sandwiching together strips of dough, as in the Chocolate and Vanilla Checkerboard Biscuits (see page 148). Brushes with smooth, fine-hair bristles and a wooden handle are ideal. Choose one that is heat-resistant and can go in the dishwasher.

## PIPING BAGS

If you can, go for large, seamless, plastic-coated **nylon** piping bags for piping biscuit dough. They have a little more weight and strength to them and don't have seams for the mixtures to leak through. They can be rinsed and then washed inside out in very hot water. Always make sure they are completely dry before putting them away. **Disposable plastic** piping bags are indispensible for piping royal icing and for finer, more detailed work and are now available in most supermarkets in the baking aisle. If you are in desperate need or for smaller jobs in which you don't need to pipe with precision, you can snip the corner off a plastic food bag to use as a piping bag. You can use the bag without a nozzle or snip a larger hole and include a nozzle.

## PIPING NOZZLES

These conical tubes fit into the end of piping bags and come in scores of different shapes and sizes, from the finest writing tip to large, sharp-toothed star nozzles, for different aesthetic and practical purposes. Although they're usually used for icing and decorating cakes, some biscuit recipes will also call for a plain nozzle, as the uncooked biscuit dough is piped into lines before baking. Boxed sets usually provide the best value, but you can start with a small selection that includes a plain 1cm nozzle and a star. Stainless-steel nozzles are the most durable, but plastic ones are also good.

## ROLLING PIN

A good rolling pin should be heavy and big enough to roll out a full batch of dough at once; solid wooden pins are easier to use than old-fashioned ones with handles. Look after your rolling pin and it should last a lifetime, so never leave a wooden rolling pin soaking in washing-up water, don't put it in the dishwasher and don't use it for anything other than rolling out dough or pastry – which means no crushing ice or tenderising meat with it!

## SCALES

Baking is really a science, so it pays to be accurate if you want perfect results every time. As you'll be dealing with some quite small quantities, **digital** scales are preferable to spring, or balance, scales as they are much more precise and can weigh ingredients that are as little as 1 gram. You can see the weight easily at a glance and you can add multiple items to one bowl simply by resetting the balance to zero after adding each ingredient. A helpful tip: always keep a spare battery on standby.

## SIEVE

Fine-mesh sieves for sifting dry ingredients will not only rid your mixture of lumps, but are the first step to combining, and aerating, dry ingredients. A sieve with a large bowl will be the most useful, but it's also handy to have a tea-strainer size for dusting icing sugar or cocoa over your finished bakes. Stainless steel is the best option.

## SPATULA

A good-quality, heat-resistant rubber or plastic spatula is really useful for thoroughly combining your ingredients, cleaning out bowls and spreading mixtures. A smaller one is a useful extra, too.

## STORAGE CONTAINERS

You don't need to buy expensive ones, but dishwasher-proof containers with secure locking clips are a good purchase. Otherwise, use a stainless-steel tin with a tight-fitting lid, or a heavy-duty plastic container with a secure lid. Store your biscuits in them well away from any heat sources (radiators, sunlight, kitchen light fittings, your fridge or cooker) and mark the container with a dated sticker so that you know when your biscuits are still good to eat.

## TIMER

A digital timer is essential for biscuit-baking. It's easy to get distracted and suddenly 10 minutes has become 15 and you have several trays of burnt biscuits. Go for a timer with seconds as well as minutes, as well as a loud ring, and set it for 1 minute less than the suggested time in the recipe, especially if you are unsure of your oven temperature – you can always increase the cooking time if needed.

## WHISKS AND MIXERS

These range from the most basic, which means the baker has to do the energetic whisking, to free-standing food mixers that do it all for you.

**Wire whisks** can be balloon-shaped or flat. A sturdy, classic hand-held whisk with an easy-grip handle makes light work of whisking eggs and whipping cream. You might find a mini/magic hand whisk is useful for stirring small quantities, for lightly beating eggs or for smoothing out lumpy mixtures.

**Rotary whisks** with two beaters in a metal frame that are turned by hand are next up in terms of power. They're perfect for whisking egg whites, for whisking mixtures over heat (no trailing leads) and for whisking out lumps.

**Hand-held electric whisks** are more expensive, but much more powerful and can be used for more general mixing. Look for models with a set of attachments and a retractable cord for easy storage.

**Free-standing electric mixers**, although non-essential and expensive, are the workhorse in any keen baker's kitchen. Not only do they make light work of creaming mixtures, they also rub butter into flour and knead dough in half the time (and with a fraction of the effort) that it takes by hand. Most free-standing mixers come with three different attachments: a whisk for eggs, meringues and light sponge mixtures; a creamer, or paddle attachment, which is ideal for creaming butter and sugar, and for rubbing cold butter into flour (see page 23); and a dough hook, which makes short work of kneading heavy dough. They do take up worktop space but they will cut your preparation time in half.

WOODEN SPOONS

You can never have enough wooden spoons – they're heat-resistant, won't scratch non-stick pans and are ideal for beating mixtures. The handles are also invaluable for making and shaping Tuiles (see page 72). It's a good idea to keep ones for baking separate from those that are used for savoury cooking, as wooden spoons are porous and will absorb strong flavours.

# Skills

Now that you have all your ingredients and equipment ready, it's time to get baking!

The recipes in this book are designed to take you stage-by-stage through all the skills you need, from absolute beginner to baking your very own spectacular showstoppers. All the recipes tell you exactly what you need to do, step-by-step, but you'll notice that some of the baking terms are highlighted in bold, which means you can refer back to this section if you want a bit more detail, or to refresh your memory.

From basic biscuit mixes to shaping, piping and decorating skills, the following pages contain invaluable hints and tips from the experts to help you bake perfect biscuits.

## THE THREE KEY BISCUIT-MAKING TECHNIQUES

The starting point for all biscuit recipes is a dough or soft batter mixture. All the recipes in this book are made with the same simple ingredients – butter, sugar, flour and sometimes eggs, used in different ratios and with various added extras to make them unique – but all of them are made using one of three methods, each of which produces a very different biscuit.

The three methods are explained in detail here, and below each method are some examples of recipes in the book that use them. Try these and you'll soon be an expert in each technique.

### RUBBED-IN METHOD

This is the most basic method and the skill used most frequently in baking – and specifically in pastry making. The key to this method is chilled, diced butter being combined with flour without melting, creaming or adding any liquids. It can be done in a food-processor, by hand, or using a free-standing mixer fitted with the creamer/paddle attachment. Tiny little crumbs of cold butter are left in the dough once they have been rubbed in and these create little pockets of steam as it bakes, giving a crumbly and crisp, rather than chewy and dry, texture. Using warm butter to rub in would make the dough greasy, tough and hard to bind together, and you'd probably need to add more liquid to bind it. Any liquid added to rubbed-in dough later on also needs to be cold, to prevent melting the butter.

*Learn with: Garibaldi Biscuits (page 76), Custard Creams (page 106) and Gingerbread House (page 154)*

**How to rub in by hand**

**1.** Sift the flour, plus any raising agents and/or spices, into a large mixing bowl. Add the cold, diced butter.

**2.** Using either a palette knife or round-bladed knife, cut the butter through the flour into smaller pieces so that the butter is covered with flour. (Or toss the butter with your fingertips to cover it in the flour.)

**3.** Use your fingers to lift up some flour and butter in both hands, allowing it to fall back into the bowl while gently pressing and rolling the butter pieces between your fingertips and thumbs. Repeat until there are no visible flecks of butter remaining, and the mixture is the texture of light sand (*see photo, right*).

**4.** Mix in your sugar, then make a well in the middle of the mixture and add any liquid and/or egg. Use the palette knife again to flick the dry ingredients into the middle of the wet ingredients and then continue mixing with your knife by gently cutting and mixing the dough to combine. (Or just use your fingers.)

**5.** When the dough starts to lump together, use your hands to gently gather it into a smooth ball, but take care not to overwork the dough as this will stretch the gluten, resulting in a tough finish to your bake.

**How to rub in using a food-processor**

**1.** Tip the flour into your food-processor bowl, add the chilled, diced butter and pulse in short bursts until there are no visible butter pieces remaining.

**2.** Add the sugar and pulse again until combined, then slowly pour the liquid through the feeder tube, pulsing until the dough starts to clump together.

**3.** Tip into a bowl and use your hands to very gently knead and gather the dough into a ball.

**How to rub in using a free-standing mixer**
1. Fit the machine with the creamer/paddle attachment and slowly mix your dry ingredients with the chilled, diced butter until the butter is no longer visible.
2. Add the sugar and mix again. You can then add the liquid and gently mix until starting to clump together.
3. Gather the dough into a smooth ball, flatten into a disc, wrap up in clingfilm and chill.

MELT AND MIX METHOD
This is a wonderfully simple one-pan technique where diced butter is gently melted in a saucepan along with sugar, and often another sweetener like honey or golden syrup. Most of the recipes using this method have a high sugar to flour (and also sometimes fat to flour) ratio, which would make rubbing-in or creaming tricky. This method is used when you want a chewy, sticky biscuit.
1. Put the diced butter and sugar (plus any other sweetener) in a pan over a low heat and stir almost constantly until the butter has melted, the sugar has completely dissolved, and the mixture is smooth (*see photo, left*).
2. Remove the pan from the heat and leave it to cool for a minute or two before adding the dry ingredients directly to the pan.
3. Mix well with a wooden spoon or rubber spatula until everything is evenly combined and coated in the butter and sugar mixture.
*Learn with: Florentines (page 88) and Brandy Snaps (page 126)*

## CREAMED METHOD

This method produces a smoother, more even texture, without the crumbly shortness of a rubbed-in dough. You can use a wooden spoon or electric whisk in a mixing bowl, or a free-standing mixer fitted with a creamer/paddle attachment. The butter and eggs (if using) should always be at room temperature so that they combine easily with the sugar – caster and icing sugars are most often used for creaming as they combine quickly and give even, consistent bakes. The result is a dense biscuit with a crisp exterior and a more robust, chewier centre.

**1.** Put the butter in a large bowl (or the bowl of a free-standing mixer), add the sugar and beat until light, pale and silky smooth (*see photo, right*) – this can take 2–3 minutes using a mixer or electric whisk, twice as long using muscle power. Whichever method you are using, you'll need to scrape down the sides of the mixing bowl with a rubber spatula from time to time, to ensure the ingredients are combined evenly.

**2.** Lightly beat the eggs (if using) in a small jug or cup before gradually adding them to the bowl, about a tablespoon at a time – mix well after each addition and scrape down the sides of the mixing bowl to make sure your ingredients are incorporated.

**3.** Sift the dry ingredients into the bowl and gently mix or **fold** in with a large metal spoon or rubber spatula, until smooth.

*Learn with: Classic Chocolate Chip Cookies (page 46), Almond, Pistachio and Rosewater Biscuits (page 100) and Chocolate and Vanilla Checkerboard Biscuits (page 148).*

## EXPERT ADVICE FROM START TO FINISH

This section takes you through every stage of the biscuit-making process, explaining the how, what and why behind the key techniques.

### HOW TO LINE A BAKING TIN OR BAKING SHEET

All the recipes in this book require a baking paper-lined baking sheet or tin. Baking paper has a non-stick coating that prevents your bakes sticking to it (or the tin) during cooking. It can be white or brown in colour and shouldn't be confused with greaseproof paper, which is an entirely different beast and is used for wrapping food.

Tear off a sheet of baking paper the same size as your baking sheet and lay it flat on the surface of the sheet. For items that need spreading or piping, or that are light and delicate, it is a useful trick to stick each corner of the paper down onto the baking sheet with a dab of mixture (*see photo, left*), but this is not necessary for more substantial bakes. It's always best to use a clean sheet of paper for each batch you bake.

### HOW TO WHISK

When making macarons and other biscuits that have a base of eggs and sugar you'll need good whisking skills. Whisking incorporates air into a mixture to create a light batter that holds its structure once cooked. It can be done in three different ways: by hand, using a balloon or rotary whisk, mixing bowl and muscle power; using an electric hand-held whisk; or in a free-standing mixer fitted with a whisk attachment. If you're whisking by hand, a large whisk will make light work of creating large pockets of air.

If you like, you can rest a medium-large mixing bowl on a damp tea towel to prevent the bowl slipping and sliding across the work surface, otherwise you can simply hold the whisk firmly in one hand and the bowl with the other. With a movement that starts at the elbow rather than the shoulder, work your whisk in rapid, large circular movements through the mixture, trying to incorporate as much air as possible as you do so. You may find it easier to tilt the bowl at an angle towards the whisk (*see photo, right*). Scrape down the sides of your bowl with a rubber spatula from time to time to ensure everything is evenly incorporated.

## HOW TO FOLD IN

When adding dried fruit, nuts or chocolate chips to biscuit or cookie dough, they'll need to be thoroughly and evenly incorporated by folding in with a large metal spoon or a sturdy rubber spatula. Using a large, deep, almost cutting action, lift the dough up from the bottom of the bowl, and over the dry ingredients. Turn the bowl clockwise slightly, and repeat this cutting, lifting and folding until the additions are evenly distributed.

It's always best to rinse glacé cherries of any sticky syrup and pat them dry on kitchen paper before using. Nuts should be toasted early on so that they can cool to room temperature before being added to the dough.

Most added extras such as nuts, dried fruit and chocolate chips are added to the dough just before the flour is completely incorporated, to reduce the chances of over-mixing the dough, which would result in tough and chewy biscuits. You should stop mixing as soon as the ingredients are evenly distributed.

## HOW TO SHAPE YOUR BISCUITS

Biscuits come in all shapes and sizes and there are various techniques used to create each one.

### How to hand-roll biscuits into balls

This is a great technique for simple, neat, but freeform cookie doughs, where chunks or spoonfuls of (often chilled) dough are rolled into neat, smooth balls between the palms of your hand (*see photo, left*). To make sure your biscuits are evenly sized (and will therefore bake to a consistent colour) you can roll one ball, weigh it and then make sure that all subsequent balls are the same weight. Always use cool, clean hands for rolling biscuit dough into balls, but if your dough is on the sticky side you can lightly dust your hands with a little flour.

### How to shape dough into a log

This technique enables you to make 'cut and come again' dough – unbaked logs can be stored in the fridge for a few days (or weeks in the freezer) and sliced and baked as needed, meaning you can bake a few or a whole batch of biscuits at any one time. Before slicing frozen dough, defrost it slowly in the fridge and slice it while it is still cold.

### How to shape a log

1. Once the dough is mixed, divide it into two even portions (you can freeze the second log after step 4 if you don't want to bake it now).

2. Using your hands, squeeze the dough into a rough, fat sausage shape so that there are no air pockets in the middle, then roll the dough on the work surface into a smooth, even log – if the dough is very sticky, it helps to lightly dust your hands with a little plain flour.

**3.** When the dough log has reached the right width, lay it on a piece of clingfilm, fold the clingfilm over to completely encase the log and twist the ends to seal it up like a Christmas cracker (*see photo, below left*).

**4.** You can then gently roll the log, holding the twisted ends of clingfilm, back and forwards a couple of times along the work surface to further smooth it.

**5.** Pop the wrapped dough logs in the freezer on a flat surface for at least 20–30 minutes to firm up the dough and ensure that the logs keep their shape when cutting. Store them in the fridge or freezer until needed.

**6.** When you want to bake your biscuits, all you need to do is unwrap the dough and, using a sharp kitchen knife, slice the log into discs of the thickness required for the recipe (usually 3–5mm). If you find that your dough is still sticky, you can simply dust the knife blade with a little plain flour between each cut.

**How to stamp out shapes using a cutter**

This technique results in perfectly uniform biscuits. Evenly roll out the dough on a lightly floured work surface to the thickness required by your recipe. Place the cutter as close as possible to one edge and stamp out a shape. If the dough is slightly sticky you can dip the bottom of the cutter into plain flour before stamping out shapes. Press the cutter into the dough using your hands, applying even pressure across the cutter to create neat biscuits with straight sides. Cut as close as possible to previous stamps to get the maximum number of biscuits from the dough at one time (*see photo, right*). Gather the off-cuts into a neat smooth ball and re-roll it so that you can stamp out more biscuits.

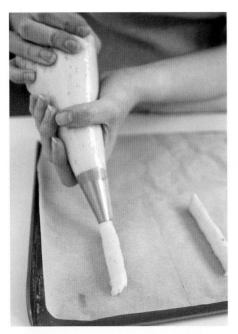

### How to pipe even-sized biscuits

To pipe your delicate piped finger biscuits to a uniform size you will need to be either very precise with your piping – practice makes perfect, which is a great excuse for making lots of batches – or you can make life easier by drawing markers on your baking paper. Using a ruler and pencil, measure out two sets of parallel lines on each sheet of baking paper, each 9cm apart. Flip the paper over so that you can still see the lines through the paper from the other side (so that you don't get any pencil or ink on your biscuits). Pipe the biscuits into fingers between your parallel lines (*see photo, left*).

### How to portion dough for chocolate chip cookies

Chocolate chip dough needs to be divided accurately to give even-sized bakes as this dough is much softer than other shaped or cut biscuits. For absolute perfection you can weigh each mound of dough, but for ease simply scoop the dough with a tablespoon or ice-cream scoop as if you were serving ice cream and arrange the mounds on prepared baking sheets, allowing plenty of space between each cookie for them to spread during baking (*see photo, left*).

### HOW TO TELL WHEN YOUR BISCUITS ARE READY

Most recipes will tell you how your bakes should look and feel when they're ready to come out of the oven. Keep an eye on them, as they near the end of the baking time, and bear in mind that some cookies may appear to be still soft after the baking time is up but will firm up quite considerably on cooling. This particularly applies to flapjacks, and cookies or biscuits with a high sugar or butter content.

## MELTING CHOCOLATE

Melting chocolate isn't tricky, but it needs a little preparation and patience. Finely chop your chocolate to ensure it melts quickly and evenly, or use good-quality chocolate chips (not to be confused with the chocolate chips that are used for cookies – these are often chocolate of a lower quality, with a higher sugar and lower cocoa content).

When melting white chocolate, try not to overheat it – white chocolate pieces may keep their shape even when the chocolate is melted because of the high fat and sugar content. If you do happen to scorch the chocolate as you melt it, it will become greasy, grainy (known as 'seizing') and unusable. Dark chocolates with a very high cocoa solid content (more than 70 per cent) and sugary white chocolate are more delicate and prone to overheating and seizing. It's not generally recommended to melt chocolate in the microwave as you will have less control over the temperature.

### How to melt chocolate

**1.** Tip the chocolate into a heatproof bowl that fits snugly over a saucepan of gently simmering water – the bottom of the bowl should not come into contact with the water below.

**2.** Leave the chocolate to melt in the heat from the water for a couple of minutes (*see photo, right*) and then gently stir with a spoon or spatula until it is completely glossy and smooth. It's ready to use as melted chocolate as soon as it is smooth and liquid – at around 30°C (86°F).

**3.** Some recipes might need the chocolate to cool slightly to prevent it melting any butter in your dough.

## HOW TO DIP BISCUITS IN CHOCOLATE

To chocolate-coat the top of biscuits, melt the chocolate following the instructions on page 31. Remove the bowl from the heat, stir until smooth and leave to cool slightly. Take one biscuit at a time, hold it at the edges with the tips of your fingers and dip the flat top evenly into the chocolate. Hold the biscuit above the bowl to let any excess chocolate drip back into the bowl – the chocolate should evenly and smoothly coat the surface of the biscuit (*see photo, left*). Lay the biscuits, chocolate-side-up, on a wire cooling rack or baking paper-lined baking sheet until the chocolate has set.

## FILLING PIPING BAGS

The recipes in this book use two types of piping bag: disposable and large nylon plastic-coated bags. Disposable piping bags are more often used when you are working with small quantities of batter or icing and/ or you need to pipe fine lines or shapes. The larger nylon bags are better for piping larger quantities, or batters such as macarons or sponge fingers (see pages 138 or 70).

**How to fill a piping bag**

**1.** For a large plastic-coated piping bag, drop the nozzle, if you are using one, into the piping bag, then snip off enough of the tip so the nozzle fits snugly and just peeps out.
**2.** Twist the bag right above the nozzle (so the filling doesn't ooze out while you're filling it), then put the bag in a tall container and fold the top of the bag over the rim so the bag is supported and easier to fill).
**3.** Spoon the filling into the bag to about two-thirds full (*see photo, left*).
**4.** Unfold the bag from the rim and twist the top to push the filling down to the (still

twisted) nozzle end, pushing out any air pockets, then twist it again to compact the filling and prevent it from escaping.

**5.** Untwist the nozzle end and squeeze the bag so the filling fills the nozzle. Practise the flow and shape of the filling before you begin, by squeezing a little out onto a plate.

**How to fill a disposable piping bag**

Disposable piping bags are filled in the same way but for much smaller quantities. Spoon the mixture into the bag, twist the top to seal and push the mixture towards the point end. Using sharp scissors, snip a very tiny point off the end to make a nozzle – you can always snip a bigger point if it's too small, but you'll have to throw the bag away and use another if you snip too big.

## HOW TO SANDWICH BISCUITS

Pair up your biscuits so they're evenly matched. Flip one biscuit in each pair over so the flat base is uppermost, then either pipe the filling onto the flat surface or spread it on top with a small off-set palette knife, or a spoon (*see photo, right*). Then, just top the filling-topped biscuit with its partner.

## HOW TO STORE YOUR BAKES

If you're not eating or serving a full batch of cookies and biscuits immediately, you can store them until needed. Line a plastic food storage box with a sheet of baking paper and stack the biscuits in layers with baking paper in between each one. Cover with a tight-fitting, secure lid.

Most biscuits will keep for up to a week in an airtight box or tin, but thinner, delicate wafer biscuits like brandy snaps or iced biscuits will start to soften after a couple of days – they'll still be delicious, but perhaps not quite as perfect.

# Help!

No matter how many biscuits you've baked in your lifetime, sometimes things will just go wrong. But don't worry, here are the most frequently encountered baking pitfalls, and how to avoid them.

## MY BISCUITS AREN'T BAKING EVENLY!

Many ovens have hot spots. You can make sure that each tray of biscuits or cookies bakes to an even colour and crispness by rotating the baking tray halfway through baking – if you're baking two trays at a time, swap them from one shelf to the other.

It can also help to double-check the temperature of your oven. Oven thermometers either sit on, or hook onto, the oven shelf, and give an accurate reading of the temperature in a particular spot so you can check for hot spots and your overall oven temperature.

## MY BISCUITS ARE UNEVENLY SIZED!

To ensure that each and every biscuit is equally sized, weigh the first scoop of dough, then match each subsequent scoop to it. If your uneven sizing happens with sandwich biscuits, you'll need to match the biscuits together as best you can, and hope you have an even number of oddly sized ones to pair up. This could be a result of not measuring your biscuits evenly if you used a ruler rather than cutter to make the shapes; chilling your rolled and cut biscuits before baking can help, too.

## CREAMING BUTTER SEEMS TO TAKE FOREVER AND IT WON'T CREAM SMOOTHLY!

It could be that your butter is too cold – this can happen even if you've left the butter out overnight to soften if your kitchen is on the cool side. Simply pop the butter in the microwave for a few seconds (in a microwave-safe bowl) on a medium heat to soften slightly.

If you've already started creaming you can still do this, as long as you haven't added the eggs. Failing that, take your time over creaming the mixture – the butter will eventually soften and cream smoothly and evenly.

## MY BISCUITS ARE STICKING TO THE BAKING PAPER!

Check that you are using baking parchment/non-stick baking paper to line your trays and not greaseproof paper. They look similar but behave very differently: bakes will stick like crazy to greaseproof paper during cooking but will easily lift off baking parchment. If you do happen to mix them up and your biscuits have got stuck, cut them off carefully with a knife and disguise the ragged bases by spreading with a buttercream filling or dipping them in melted chocolate (see page 32).

## MY DOUGH IS TOO SOFT TO ROLL OUT AND STAMP OUT SHAPES!

Give yourself a little extra time and set the dough in the fridge for 30–60 minutes, or in the freezer for 20 minutes to chill.

## MY CUTTERS ARE STICKING TO THE DOUGH AS I CUT OUT SHAPES!

If your dough is on the sticky or soft side, you might find the cutter sticks as you stamp out shapes. This is easily solved by dipping the cutter in plain flour in between each stamping.

## MY BISCUITS HAVE SPREAD DURING COOKING AND MERGED INTO ONE!

Try to leave plenty of space between each of your biscuits or cookies to allow room for them to spread. If, however, your bake has spread so that you have one large biscuit instead of 12, simply cut the still-warm bake into pieces – if you wait until they cool, the biscuit will crumble. Which is another solution: crumble the biscuit into chunks and you have a fancy cheesecake base, or fold it into melted dark chocolate along with a handful of mini marshmallows, glacé cherries and some chopped nuts. Press the whole lot into a lined tin, leave in the fridge until set and – voila! – tasty tiffin.

## ICING DISASTER!

If you're unsure of your icing skills, have a practice run on some parchment paper before committing your design to the baked biscuits. Feathered icing (see Lemon Butter Cookies on page 80) is a brilliant way of covering a multitude of icing mistakes, but if your feathering is not as delicate as you'd hoped, simply turn it into marbling: rather than dragging the point of a wooden skewer or cocktail stick neatly back and forth through the icing lines, be more freestyle by swirling two coloured icings.

If you do make a glaring mistake on intricately iced biscuits that absolutely cannot be rectified, just scrape the icing off with a palette knife and start again – or cover the mistake with a generous flourish of sprinkles.

# BAKE IT BETTER
## *Recipes*

# Thumbprint Cookies

These crumbly cookies couldn't be easier, with no fancy cutters or rolling out. They're fun to make with kids and can be filled with different jams for a colourful party spread.

200g unsalted butter, at room temperature
100g caster sugar
1 large egg yolk
1 teaspoon vanilla extract
275g plain flour
pinch of salt
150g raspberry jam

HANDS-ON TIME:
10 minutes,
plus 1 hour chilling

BAKING TIME:
15 minutes

MAKES:
24 biscuits

SPECIAL EQUIPMENT:
2 baking sheets

METHOD USED:
Creamed method,
page 25

1. Cream together the butter and caster sugar until really pale and light – you'll find this easiest using a free-standing mixer fitted with the creamer/paddle attachment but a hand-held mixer or bowl and wooden spoon will do just as well. Scrape down the sides of the bowl with a rubber spatula from time to time as you are working.

2. Add the egg yolk and vanilla extract and mix again until thoroughly combined. Sift the flour into the bowl with the salt and mix until the dough comes together into a smooth ball. Don't overwork the dough or the cookies could end up tough rather than crisp and crumbly. Cover the bowl with clingfilm and chill for 1 hour, until firm.

3. Preheat the oven to 180°C (160°C fan), Gas 4 and **line** two baking sheets with baking paper. Using your hands, roll the dough into walnut-sized balls and arrange on the lined baking sheets, leaving a little space between each biscuit, as they will spread slightly during cooking.

4. Using your thumb or finger, press into the middle of each cookie. Bake on the middle shelf of the oven for about 15 minutes, or until pale golden. Remove from the oven and gently press your thumb into the indent again. Fill each indent with ½–1 teaspoon of jam, depending on its depth, and return the cookies to the oven for another minute.

5. Leave to cool on the baking sheet for a few minutes, then transfer to a wire rack to cool completely.

## Try Something Different

Add the finely grated zest of 1 unwaxed lemon to the dough and fill the indent with lemon curd, or swap 15g of the plain flour for the same amount of cocoa powder and fill the indent with chocolate and hazelnut spread. Reduce the flour by 75g and add 50g ground almonds or hazelnuts and 25g of cocoa powder. Fill the indents with raspberry jam, chocolate and hazelnut spread or peanut butter.

# Flapjacks

These flapjacks are delicious and moreish and have a crunchier texture with the addition of mixed seeds. For your perfect flapjack – crunchy or chewy – follow the timings below.

100g golden syrup
100g demerara sugar
125g unsalted butter, diced
250g rolled porridge oats
75g mixed seeds (sunflower, pumpkin, golden linseed and sesame)
¼ teaspoon ground ginger
pinch of salt

HANDS-ON TIME:
10 minutes

BAKING TIME:
20–25 minutes

MAKES:
16 squares

SPECIAL EQUIPMENT:
20cm square baking tin

METHOD USED:
Melt and mix method, page 24

1. Preheat the oven to 180°C (160°C fan), Gas 4 and **line** the base and sides of the baking tin with baking paper.

2. To make it easy to measure golden syrup from a tin, first heat a tablespoon in a mug of boiling water for a minute before using. If you have digital scales, place a small pan on the scales, making sure they are registering zero, and use the hot spoon to scoop the syrup from the tin and into the pan. Re-set the scales to zero and add the demerara sugar and unsalted butter. Set the pan over a low heat to melt the butter and dissolve the sugar. Stir until smooth and remove from the heat.

3. Mix the porridge oats, mixed seeds, ginger and salt in a mixing bowl. Add the melted butter mixture and stir well to thoroughly combine. Spoon into the prepared tin and press level with the back of a spoon.

4. Bake on the middle shelf of the oven for 20–25 minutes, until starting to firm, remembering to use the shorter cooking time for more chewy flapjacks and the longer time if you prefer them crisper. The flapjacks will firm up and crisp as they cool.

5. Remove from the oven and mark the flapjack into squares. Cool in the tin on a wire rack.

## Try Something Different

Increase the amount of ground ginger to 1 tsp and add a nugget of stem ginger, finely chopped, or add 50g raisins, sultanas, chopped dates or apricots to the dry ingredients. for a thinner, crisper flapjack, bake it in a 23cm square tin for 20 minutes.

# Icebox Cookies

These are infinitely adaptable cookies – the options for added extras are endless. The dough is shaped into a neat log and sliced after chilling, so it can be prepared in advance.

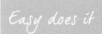

HANDS-ON TIME:
15 minutes,
plus 1 hour chilling

BAKING TIME:
12 minutes

MAKES:
about 40 biscuits

SPECIAL
EQUIPMENT:
2 baking sheets

METHOD USED:
Creamed method,
page 25

100g dried or glacé cherries, roughly chopped
225g unsalted butter, at room temperature
125g icing sugar

2 medium egg yolks
1 teaspoon vanilla extract
300g plain flour
pinch of salt

1. If you are using glacé cherries tip them into a sieve, rinse in warm water to remove any excess syrup and pat dry on kitchen paper. Roughly chop the cherries, whichever type you are using, and set aside.

2. Cream the butter and icing sugar together until pale and light, scraping down the mixing bowl from time to time with a rubber spatula. Add the egg yolks, one at a time, mixing well between each one and then add the vanilla extract.

3. Sift the flour and salt into the bowl and mix until almost combined. Add the chopped cherries and mix again until thoroughly combined. Divide the dough into two equal-sized portions. Lightly flour your work surface and hands and then **shape** each piece into a neat, smooth log, 4–5cm in diameter. Wrap tightly in clingfilm and chill for at least 1 hour, until firm.

4. Preheat the oven to 180°C (160°C fan), Gas 4 and **line** two baking sheets with baking paper.

5. Cut the logs into slices, roughly 5mm thick, and arrange on the prepared baking sheets. Bake on the middle shelf of the oven for about 12 minutes, or until firm and pale golden brown. Leave the cookies to cool on the baking sheets for a few minutes before transferring to a wire rack to cool completely.

## Try Something Different

Brush the chilled log with milk or lightly beaten egg white and roll in crushed flaked almonds or cinnamon sugar for a crisp edge to each cookie. Add finely grated orange or lemon zest and finely chopped candied peel to the dough instead of the cherries, or try adding 50g grated chocolate to the dough and roll the logs in finely chopped pistachios.

# Anzac Biscuits

These delicious biscuits are named after the Australian and New Zealand soldiers they were sent to in World War 1; with no eggs in the recipe they could withstand the voyage to Europe.

Easy does it

HANDS-ON TIME:
10 minutes

BAKING TIME:
12 minutes

MAKES:
20 biscuits

SPECIAL
EQUIPMENT:
2 baking sheets

METHOD USED:
Melt and mix
method, page 24

150g plain flour
125g porridge oats
75g desiccated coconut
50g soft light brown sugar
25g caster sugar

pinch of salt
125g unsalted butter
100g golden syrup
½ teaspoon bicarbonate of soda
2 tablespoons boiling water

1. Preheat the oven to 180°C (160°C fan), Gas 4 and **line** two baking sheets with baking paper.

2. In a large mixing bowl stir together the flour, oats, coconut, soft light brown sugar, caster sugar and salt.

3. Melt the butter and golden syrup together in a small pan set over a low heat (or in the microwave on a low-medium setting). Remove the pan from the heat, add the bicarbonate of soda and boiling water and quickly mix with a whisk to combine.

4. Pour the melted butter mixture into the dry ingredients and mix with a wooden spoon or rubber spatula until thoroughly combined. Using your hands, roll level tablespoons of the mixture into walnut-sized balls and arrange on the prepared baking sheets, leaving plenty of space between each one as they will spread during cooking. Using the back of a spoon, slightly flatten each biscuit and bake in batches on the middle shelf of the oven for about 12 minutes, until almost firm and starting to crisp. The biscuits will crisp and firm up more as they cool.

5. Leave the biscuits on the trays for a few minutes, then transfer to a wire rack to cool completely.

Try Something Different

Add a handful of pumpkin, sunflower or sesame seeds to the mixture, or use coconut sugar instead of the soft light brown sugar.

# Classic Chocolate Chip Cookies

In a twist on the classic recipe, here hazelnuts are baked with a generous helping of chocolate chips. Preparing the dough 24 hours before baking gives a better texture and shape.

100g blanched hazelnuts
200g unsalted butter, at room temperature
125g soft light brown sugar
100g caster sugar
2 medium eggs, lightly beaten
1 teaspoon vanilla extract

275g plain flour
½ teaspoon bicarbonate of soda
¼ teaspoon baking powder
pinch of salt
200g chocolate chips (dark or milk or a combination of both)

1. Preheat the oven to 180°C (160°C fan), Gas 4 and **line** two baking sheets with baking paper. Roughly chop the hazelnuts and set aside.

2. Cream the butter with the soft light brown sugar and caster sugar until pale and light – using a free-standing mixer makes light work of this but a hand-held mixer works too. Gradually add the beaten eggs, mixing well between each addition and scraping down the sides of the bowl with a rubber spatula from time to time. Add the vanilla extract and mix again.

3. Sift the plain flour, bicarbonate of soda, baking powder and salt into the bowl and mix until almost combined. Add the chocolate chips and chopped hazelnuts and mix again until they are evenly distributed throughout the dough. If you like, you can now chill the dough for up to 24 hours until ready to bake.

4. Portion the dough to create biscuits of an even size – a good tip is to use an ice-cream scoop or tablespoon to drop even-sized mounds of dough onto the baking sheets. Leave plenty of space between each to allow the cookies to spread during cooking. Flatten the cookies slightly using your fingers and bake on the middle shelf of the oven for 12 minutes, until the cookies are lightly browned but the middle is still slightly soft. They will crisp up more as they cool.

5. Leave to cool on the baking sheets for 5 minutes, then use a palette knife or fish slice to transfer to a wire rack to cool completely.

## Try Something Different

Replace the hazelnuts with macadamia nuts and use white chocolate chips. For a chunkier cookie, roughly chop a 200g bar of chocolate instead of using chocolate chips.

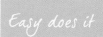

*Easy does it*

HANDS-ON TIME:
15 minutes,
plus overnight
chilling

BAKING TIME:
12 minutes

MAKES:
24 biscuits

SPECIAL
EQUIPMENT:
2 baking sheets

METHOD USED:
Creamed method,
page 25

# Oatmeal Raisin Cookies

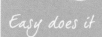

These cookies may be loaded with good stuff but are still deliciously sweet and chewy. Use whole rolled oats for a better flavour and texture rather than quick-cook porridge oats.

225g unsalted butter, at room temperature
200g soft light brown sugar
50g soft dark brown sugar
1 teaspoon vanilla extract
2 large eggs, lightly beaten
175g plain flour
1 teaspoon bicarbonate of soda

½ teaspoon ground cinnamon
good pinch of salt
200g rolled porridge oats
150g raisins
100g pecans, roughly chopped
50g desiccated coconut
50g mixed seeds (sunflower, pumpkin, sesame and golden linseed)

*Easy does it*

HANDS-ON TIME:
15 minutes,
plus 1 hour chilling

MAKES:
about 30 biscuits

BAKING TIME:
12–14 minutes

SPECIAL EQUIPMENT:
2 baking sheets

METHOD USED:
Creamed method,
page 25

1. Cream the butter with the light and dark brown sugars in a free-standing mixer until pale and light – this will take about 3 minutes. Scrape down the insides of the bowl from time to time so that all of the ingredients are thoroughly incorporated. Add the vanilla extract and mix again.

2. Gradually add the beaten eggs, mixing well between each addition. Sift the flour, bicarbonate of soda, ground cinnamon and a good pinch of salt into the bowl and mix until barely combined. Add the oats, raisins, chopped pecans, coconut and seeds and mix again until all of the ingredients are thoroughly incorporated. Cover the bowl with clingfilm and chill for 1 hour.

3. Preheat the oven to 180°C (160°C fan), Gas 4 and **line** two baking sheets with baking paper.

4. Scoop level tablespoons of dough into balls and place on the prepared baking sheets, leaving plenty of space between each one to allow for spreading during cooking. Flatten each cookie with your hands and bake in batches on the middle shelf of the oven for 12–14 minutes, until crisp and golden brown. The cookies are better when slightly soft and chewy, and as they crisp up as they cool, don't overcook them.

5. Remove from the oven and leave on the baking sheets for 2–3 minutes to firm up, then transfer the cookies to a wire cooling rack using a palette knife or fish slice. These cookies can be rolled into balls and frozen in bags, then baked from frozen or defrosted first.

## Try Something Different

Swap the raisins with other dried fruit, depending on your tastes and what you have in your store cupboard – sultanas make a delicious alternative, or use walnuts instead of pecans. Try using coconut sugar in place of the soft light brown sugar for a hint of coconut as well as a more caramelly flavour.

# Gingerbread Men

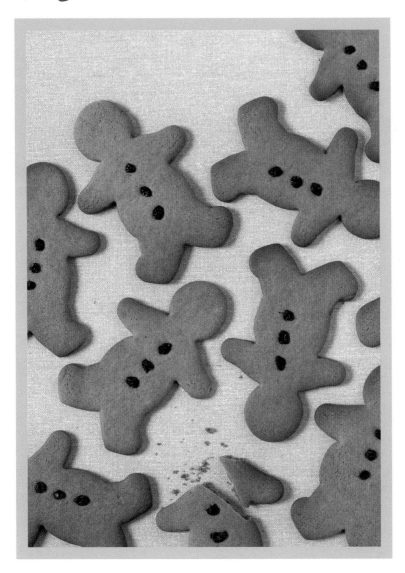

These nostalgic biscuits are ideal for making with children. You can easily get classic gingerbread men cutters, but look out for gingerbread ladies and children for the whole family.

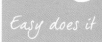

*Easy does it*

HANDS-ON TIME:
10 minutes

BAKING TIME:
12 minutes

MAKES:
10–12 biscuits

SPECIAL
EQUIPMENT:
2 baking sheets,
gingerbread man
cookie cutter

METHOD USED:
Rubbed-in method,
page 22

2 tablespoons golden syrup
1 large egg yolk
200g plain flour, plus extra for rolling
½ teaspoon bicarbonate of soda
2 teaspoons ground ginger
1 teaspoon ground cinnamon

½ teaspoon mixed spice
pinch of salt
100g unsalted butter, chilled and diced
75g light muscovado sugar
currants, to decorate

1. Preheat the oven to 180°C (160°C fan), Gas 4 and **line** two baking sheets with baking paper.

2. Mix together the golden syrup and egg yolk in a small bowl.

3. Tip the flour, bicarbonate of soda, ginger, ground cinnamon, mixed spice and salt into a large bowl and add the diced butter. **Rub** the butter into the flour using your fingers but trying not to overwork the mixture. You can also do this step in a food-processor or in a free-standing mixer fitted with the creamer/paddle attachment.

4. When the mixture resembles fine sand and there are no visible lumps of butter remaining, add the light muscovado sugar and mix again to incorporate. Add the golden syrup and egg yolk mixture and mix again until the dough starts to clump together. Use your hands to gently knead the dough into a smooth ball.

5. Lightly dust the work surface with flour and roll the dough out to a thickness of 2–3mm. Using the gingerbread man cutter, stamp out **shapes** from the dough and carefully arrange on the prepared baking sheets, leaving a little space between each cookie. Gather any dough scraps together and knead gently into a ball, re-roll and stamp out more cookies. Press 3–4 currants onto each gingerbread man for buttons and bake on the middle shelf of the oven for about 12 minutes, until starting to brown slightly at the edges.

6. Leave to cool and firm up on the baking sheets for 5 minutes before transferring to a wire rack to cool completely.

# Spiced Apple Cookies

The secret ingredient in these soft, moreish cookies makes them an ideal bake for those following a vegan diet – thick apple purée replaces eggs and sunflower oil replaces butter.

HANDS-ON TIME:
15 minutes

BAKING TIME:
10 minutes

MAKES:
24 biscuits

SPECIAL
EQUIPMENT:
2 baking sheets

METHOD USED:
Melt and mix
method, page 24

175g thick apple purée or good-quality ready-made apple sauce
100ml sunflower oil
50g dark treacle
125g light muscovado sugar
75g raisins or sultanas
300g plain flour

½ teaspoon baking powder
1 teaspoon bicarbonate of soda
1 teaspoon ground ginger
2 teaspoons ground cinnamon
good grating of nutmeg
pinch of salt
100g granulated sugar, for rolling

1. Heat the apple purée in a small pan over a low heat for a minute to cook off any excess liquid. Tip into a medium bowl, add the sunflower oil, treacle, light muscovado sugar and raisins or sultanas. Mix to combine and leave to cool to room temperature.

2. Preheat the oven to 180°C (160°C fan), Gas 4 and **line** two baking sheets with baking paper.

3. Sift the flour, baking powder, bicarbonate of soda, ginger, cinnamon, nutmeg and salt into the bowl with the apple and treacle mixture and stir well until thoroughly combined.

4. Tip the granulated sugar and remaining cinnamon onto a large plate or tray. Using a dessertspoon and your hands, scoop walnut-sized balls of dough into balls and roll in the cinnamon sugar to completely coat. Arrange on the prepared baking sheets, leaving plenty of space between each cookie to spread during baking, and flatten slightly with your fingers.

5. Bake on the middle shelf of the oven for 10 minutes, until the top of the cookies are crisp. Leave to cool on the baking sheets for 5 minutes and then transfer to a wire rack to cool completely.

*Try Something Different*

The dark treacle can easily be swapped for blackstrap molasses if that is what you happen to have to hand – molasses will give a slightly warmer, toffee-ish flavour. Add a finely chopped nugget of stem ginger or a handful of chopped pecans with the dry ingredients. Mix 1–2 tbsp of maple syrup with about 150g icing sugar to make a drizzly icing to zigzag over the cookies.

# Shortbread

Crumbly, light and buttery shortbread is a good introduction to using different flours – cornflour gives a more delicate crumb, while rice flour adds a slight grittiness.

125g unsalted butter, at room temperature
50g caster sugar, plus 1 tablespoon
150g plain flour, plus extra for dusting
50g cornflour or rice flour
pinch of salt

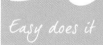
HANDS-ON TIME:
10 minutes,
plus 1 hour chilling

BAKING TIME:
45 minutes

SERVES:
8

SPECIAL
EQUIPMENT:
baking tray

METHOD USED:
Creamed method,
page 25

1. Cream the butter with the caster sugar until pale and light – this is easiest in a free-standing mixer fitted with the creamer/paddle attachment. Scrape down the sides of the bowl with a rubber spatula from time to time.

2. Add the plain flour, cornflour (or rice flour) and salt and mix to combine, but don't overwork the dough.

3. Very lightly dust a sheet of baking paper with plain flour and press or roll the dough into a 20cm disc – you can use a cake tin as a guide to get it really neat. Carefully lift the shortbread dough, still on its paper, onto the middle of a baking sheet. Use your fingers to crimp the shortbread circle, making a decorative pattern around the edges. Use a knife to mark the shortbread into eight equal sections, but do not cut all the way through the dough. Prick with a fork and chill for 30 minutes to 1 hour while you preheat the oven to 150°C (130°C fan), Gas 2.

4. Bake the shortbread on the middle shelf of the oven for about 45 minutes to 1 hour, until light golden. Remove from the oven, sprinkle with the extra caster sugar and leave to cool on the baking sheet for 10 minutes, then carefully slide onto a wire rack to cool completely. Cut into sections to serve.

## Try Something Different

Use vanilla sugar instead of regular caster or add the seeds from 1 vanilla pod when creaming the butter and sugar, or swap regular caster for golden caster sugar for slightly more crumbly shortbread with a faint hint of caramel. Add 1 tbsp of finely chopped candied peel and the finely grated zest of ½ unwaxed lemon.

# Cheese and Sun-Dried Tomato Sables

Crisp and cheesey, these bite-sized biscuits are perfect served with drinks or as canapés – perhaps topped with a little pesto, cherry tomato and goat's cheese.

*Easy does it*

HANDS-ON TIME:
15 minutes,
plus 2 hours chilling

BAKING TIME:
12–15 minutes

MAKES:
30 biscuits

SPECIAL
EQUIPMENT:
2 baking sheets

75g sun-dried tomatoes in oil (drained weight)
100g plain flour
75g white spelt flour
½ teaspoon sea salt
good pinch of cayenne pepper
good pinch of English mustard powder
I teaspoon caraway seeds, lightly crushed

125g unsalted butter, chilled and diced
50g mature Cheddar, finely grated
75g Parmesan, finely grated
2 tablespoons sesame seeds
I tablespoon black sesame or black onion (nigella) seeds
I tablespoon milk
freshly ground black pepper

1. Pat the drained sun-dried tomatoes with kitchen paper to remove as much oil as possible. Chop into small pieces and set aside.

2. Tip the plain flour, spelt flour, salt, cayenne pepper, mustard powder and caraway seeds into the bowl of a food-processor and season with a good grind of black pepper. Add the diced butter and, using the pulse button, mix the butter into the dry ingredients until there are no visible flecks of butter remaining.

3. Add the grated Cheddar and Parmesan and pulse again until the dough just starts to come together in clumps. Add the sun-dried tomatoes and pulse again to combine.

4. Tip the dough into a bowl and use your hands to bring it together into a smooth ball. Lightly flour your hands and **shape** the dough into a log, roughly 5cm in diameter, by rolling it on a clean work surface. Wrap tightly in clingfilm and chill for 2 hours, or until firm.

5. Preheat the oven to 180°C (160°C fan), Gas 4 and **line** two baking sheets with baking paper.

6. Mix the sesame seeds and black sesame or onion seeds together on a tray. Unwrap the sablé logs, brush with the milk and roll in the seeds, pressing them into the dough so that they stick evenly. Slice the logs into discs, around 5mm thick, and arrange on the baking sheets, spacing them well apart.

7. Bake on the middle shelf of the oven for 12–15 minutes, or until crisp and golden. Leave to rest on the baking sheets for 2 minutes, then transfer to a wire rack to cool. **Store** in an airtight container for up to 4 days and reheat in a moderate oven to crisp up.

*Try Something Different*

Swap the sun-dried tomatoes for the same amount of chopped black olives or replace the caraway seeds in the dough with cumin or fennel seeds. Roll the logs in poppy seeds instead of sesame and black onion seeds.

# Oatmeal Biscuits for Cheese

These lightly spiced, crumbly biscuits are ideal to serve alongside cheeses. For a perfect crumbly texture, don't overwork the dough as it will stretch the gluten in the flour.

100g medium oatmeal
175g wholegrain spelt flour
2 teaspoons baking powder
2 teaspoons mustard powder
1 teaspoon coarsely ground black pepper
¼ teaspoon cayenne pepper
1 teaspoon sea salt flakes, plus extra for sprinkling

125g unsalted butter, chilled and diced
2 tablespoons soft light brown sugar
2 teaspoons poppy seeds, plus extra for sprinkling
3 tablespoons whole milk
plain flour for dusting

*Easy does it*

HANDS-ON TIME:
10 minutes

BAKING TIME:
12 minutes

MAKES:
30–40 biscuits

SPECIAL EQUIPMENT:
2 baking sheets

METHOD USED
Rubbed-in method, page 22

1. Preheat the oven to 170°C (150°C fan), Gas 3 and **line** two baking sheets with baking paper.

2. Sift the oatmeal, spelt flour, baking powder, mustard powder, pepper and cayenne into a large bowl. Tip any bran left in the sieve back into the bowl. Add the salt and diced butter and, using your hands, **rub** the butter into the flour.

3. When there are no visible flecks of butter remaining and the mixture resembles damp sand, add the sugar and poppy seeds and mix again to combine. Add the milk and mix into the dry ingredients using a palette knife, until the dough starts to clump together and then use your hands to gently bring the dough into a neat ball. Do not over-work the dough otherwise your biscuits will be tough rather than crisp.

4. Lightly dust the work surface with plain flour and **roll** out the dough out to a thickness of no more than 2mm. Cut into neat 6–7cm squares and arrange on the lined baking sheets. Gather the dough scraps together, re-roll and cut out more biscuits. Prick each biscuit with a fork, sprinkle with a little salt flakes and/or poppy seeds and bake on the middle shelf of the oven for about 12 minutes, until lightly golden and crisp.

5. Transfer to a wire rack to cool.

*Try Something Different*

Use smoked sea salt flakes instead of regular flakes. Add a teaspoon of finely chopped fresh rosemary or thyme. You can also make the dough using a food-processor if you prefer and stamp out the biscuits using a round or square cookie cutter.

# Coconut, Almond and Date Cookies

These wholesome biscuits are not only very tasty but are packed with goodness, too. Coconut oil is a new favourite and is available in health food stores, supermarkets and online.

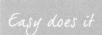

HANDS-ON TIME:
15 minutes

BAKING TIME:
10 minutes

MAKES:
about 20 biscuits

SPECIAL EQUIPMENT:
2 baking sheets

METHOD USED:
Melt and mix method, page 24

150g blanched almonds
100g coconut chips or unsweetened desiccated coconut
100g pitted medjool dates
50g coconut oil

50g coconut nectar/syrup or agave syrup
1 teaspoon vanilla extract
½ teaspoon mixed spice
pinch of salt

1. Preheat the oven to 160°C (140°C fan), Gas 3 and **line** two baking sheets with baking paper.

2. Tip the blanched almonds into a food-processor or mini blender and pulse until finely ground. Tip into a mixing bowl. Add the coconut chips to the food-processor and pulse these until very finely chopped and then add to the almonds. Repeat with the pitted dates and finely chop, almost to a paste. Add to the almonds and coconut.

3. Melt the coconut oil, either in a small pan over a low heat or in the microwave on a low setting. Add the coconut nectar (or agave syrup) and vanilla extract and pour into the mixing bowl, along with the mixed spice and salt. Mix together, at first with a spoon to combine, and then with your hands to bring all the ingredients together until thoroughly combined.

4. Using your hands, roll the mixture into neat walnut-sized balls and arrange on the lined baking sheets. Flatten into neat 1cm-thick rounds and bake on the middle shelf of the oven for about 10 minutes, until starting to turn golden at the edges. The biscuits will seem quite soft but will harden further on cooling – leave them on the baking sheet for 2–3 minutes and then transfer to a wire rack to cool completely.

*Try Something Different*

Use honey instead of the coconut nectar or agave syrup, but remember that will mean these biscuits are no longer suitable for vegans.

# Gingersnaps

These crisp biscuits pack a powerful punch, with ground ginger and chewy ginger chunks. The pinch of cayenne pepper adds extra heat, but feel free to leave it out if you prefer.

| | |
|---|---|
| 200g unsalted butter, at room temperature | 425g plain flour |
| 125g caster sugar | 2 teaspoons bicarbonate of soda |
| 175g golden syrup | 4–5 teaspoons ground ginger |
| 50g treacle | 1 teaspoon ground cinnamon |
| 1 large egg, lightly beaten | large pinch of cayenne pepper |
| 50g stem ginger in syrup, drained | pinch of salt |
| | 100g granulated sugar |

HANDS-ON TIME:
15

BAKING TIME:
12 minutes

MAKES:
30 biscuits

SPECIAL
EQUIPMENT:
2 baking sheets

METHOD USED:
Creamed method,
page 25

1. Preheat the oven to 180°C (160°C fan), Gas 4 and **line** two baking sheets with baking paper.

2. Cream together the butter and caster sugar until light and fluffy – this is easiest using a free-standing mixer fitted with a creamer/paddle attachment. Add the golden syrup, treacle and beaten egg and mix until smooth, scraping down the bowl with a rubber spatula from time to time. Finely chop the stem ginger, add to the bowl and mix again.

3. Sift the flour, bicarbonate of soda, ground ginger, ground cinnamon, cayenne pepper and salt into the bowl and mix again until thoroughly combined. Tip the granulated sugar onto a tray.

4. Using your hands, roll the gingersnap mixture into walnut-sized balls and roll in the granulated sugar to coat completely. Arrange on the prepared baking sheets, allowing plenty of space for the biscuits to spread during baking and flatten the top of each using a fork.

5. Bake in batches on the middle shelf of the oven for about 12 minutes, or until golden brown and the edges of the cookies are crisp and the middle is still slightly soft. (The gingersnaps will crisp further as they cool.) Leave the biscuits on the trays for 5 minutes and then transfer to a wire rack to cool completely.

### Try Something Different

Add 2 tsp finely grated fresh ginger to give a really powerful ginger hit to these biscuits, or for less ginger, replace the stem ginger with 1 tbsp finely chopped mixed peel. Dip the underside of each gingersnap in **melted** dark chocolate (see the recipe for Florentines, page 88, for tips on how to do this).

# Double Chocolate Peanut Butter Cookies

These delicious cookies are packed with dark and white chocolate chunks and a double dose of peanuts. The trick is not to over-bake them so they are slightly soft in the middle.

HANDS-ON TIME:
20 minutes

BAKING TIME:
12 minutes

MAKES:
24 biscuits

SPECIAL
EQUIPMENT:
2 baking sheets

METHOD USED:
Creamed method,
page 25

125g dark chocolate, preferably a minimum of 65 per cent cocoa solids, chopped
125g white chocolate
100g salted roasted peanuts
100g unsalted butter, at room temperature
125g crunchy peanut butter
225g soft light brown sugar

2 large eggs, lightly beaten
1 teaspoon vanilla extract
200g plain flour
40g cocoa powder
1 teaspoon bicarbonate of soda
½ teaspoon baking powder
pinch of salt
2 tablespoons milk

1. Preheat the oven to 170°C (150°C fan), Gas 3 and **line** two baking sheets with baking paper.

2. **Melt** the dark chocolate in a heatproof glass or ceramic bowl, either over a pan of barely simmering water, making sure the bottom of the bowl doesn't touch the water. Stir until smooth, remove from the heat and leave to cool slightly. Chop the white chocolate into chunks and very roughly chop the peanuts and put to one side.

3. Cream the butter with the peanut butter and soft light brown sugar until pale and light – this will be easiest using a free-standing mixer fitted with the creamer/paddle attachment. Gradually add the eggs, mixing well between each addition and scraping down the sides of the bowl with a rubber spatula from time to time. Add the vanilla extract and mix again.

4. Add the cooled melted chocolate and mix until smooth. Sift the flour, cocoa powder, bicarbonate of soda, baking powder and a pinch of salt into the bowl and mix until barely combined before adding the milk, white chocolate chunks and chopped peanuts. Mix again to thoroughly combine.

5. Using a tablespoon, scoop even-sized mounds onto the lined baking sheets, leaving plenty of space between each cookie to allow them to spread during baking. Bake in batches, for 10 minutes on the middle shelf of the oven. Remove from the oven and flatten each cookie slightly with a fish slice or palette knife and return to the oven for a further minute. The cookies will still be slightly soft at this point but will harden as they cool – if you can wait that long. Cool the cookies on the baking sheets for a few minutes and then transfer to a wire rack to cool completely.

# Honey and Pine Nut Cookies

Aromatic orange blossom honey adds a sweetness to these slightly soft pine nuts and candied peel cookies. Flattening them slightly before baking makes them crisp rather than cakey.

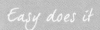
HANDS-ON TIME:
15 minutes

BAKING TIME:
12 minutes

MAKES:
24 biscuits

SPECIAL
EQUIPMENT:
2 baking sheets

METHOD USED:
Creamed method,
page 25

225g plain flour
½ teaspoon bicarbonate of soda
1 teaspoon ground cinnamon
pinch of ground allspice
pinch of ground cloves
pinch of salt
150g unsalted butter, at room temperature
150g golden caster sugar, plus 50g extra for coating

75g clear orange blossom honey, plus 1 tablespoon for brushing
finely grated zest of ½ orange
1 tablespoon orange juice
1 medium egg, lightly beaten
100g pine nuts
50g candied peel, finely chopped

1. Sift the plain flour, bicarbonate of soda, spices and salt into a bowl.

2. Cream the butter with 100g of the golden caster sugar until pale and light – this is quickest in a free-standing mixer fitted with a creamer/paddle attachment. Scrape down the sides of the mixing bowl with a rubber spatula from time to time. Gradually add the clear honey, orange zest and juice and beaten egg and mix again until smooth.

3. Tip the sifted dry ingredients into the bowl and mix again until almost combined. Add 50g of the pine nuts and 25g of the candied peel and mix until combined. Cover the bowl with clingfilm and chill for 30 minutes to help make shaping the dough easier.

4. Preheat the oven to 180°C (140°C fan), Gas 4 and **line** two baking sheets with baking paper.

5. Tip the remaining 50g caster sugar onto a tray. Scoop level tablespoons of the cookie mixture and roll into balls. Drop into the sugar, roll to coat and then arrange on the lined baking sheets, leaving space between each cookie. Flatten each one slightly with your fingers. Divide the remaining pine nuts and candied peel between the cookies, pressing slightly into the top of each, and bake on the middle shelf of the oven for 12 minutes, until golden brown, slightly risen and starting to firm at the edges.

6. Remove from the oven and brush the top of each hot cookie with a little honey. Leave to rest on the baking sheets for 3 minutes and then, using a fish slice or palette knife, transfer to a wire rack to cool completely.

## *Try Something Different*

Use chopped walnuts instead of the pine nuts, or add a teaspoon of finely chopped fresh rosemary to the mix.

# Sesame Crisps

Delicious with fresh mint tea or coffee these sesame cookies are flavoured with tahini and the merest hint of cocoa, giving them an exotic flavour that is similar to halva.

100g sesame seeds
125g unsalted butter, at room temperature
75g caster sugar
2 tablespoons clear honey or agave syrup
2 tablespoons tahini

1 teaspoon vanilla extract
150g plain flour
25g ground almonds
15g cocoa powder
½ teaspoon baking powder
pinch of salt

HANDS-ON TIME:
20 minutes, plus
1 hour chilling

BAKING TIME:
10 minutes

MAKES:
about 20 biscuits

SPECIAL
EQUIPMENT:
2 baking sheets

METHOD USED:
Creamed method,
page 25

1. Preheat the oven to 170°C (150°C fan), Gas 3 and **line** a baking sheet with baking paper. Tip the sesame seeds onto the lined baking sheet and toast in the oven for about 4 minutes, until golden – keep an eye on them as they can easily burn due to their high oil content. Remove from the oven and cool. You can turn the oven off for now.

2. Cream the butter with the caster sugar until pale and light, scraping down the sides of the mixing bowl from time to time. Add the honey (or agave syrup), tahini and vanilla extract and mix again.

3. Sift the flour, ground almonds, cocoa powder, baking powder and salt into the bowl. Add 40g of the toasted sesame seeds and mix until thoroughly combined, scraping down the bowl with a rubber spatula to ensure that the ingredients are thoroughly incorporated. Scoop the mixture into a clean bowl, cover with clingfilm and chill for 1 hour.

4. Preheat the oven to 170°C (150°C fan), Gas 3 and **line** two baking sheets with baking paper.

5. Using a dessertspoon and your hands, **roll** large cherry-sized nuggets of the dough into balls. Roll the balls in the reserved toasted sesame seeds to coat, arrange on the prepared baking sheets and flatten slightly with your hands. Allow a little space between each ball to allow them to spread during cooking. Bake the biscuits on the middle shelf of the oven for 10 minutes, until firm (they will crisp further on cooling).

6. Leave the biscuits to cool on the baking sheets for 10 minutes and then transfer to a wire rack to cool completely.

## Try Something Different

For a savoury version, replace the cocoa powder with spelt or rye flour, omit the vanilla extract and roll the balls in za'atar instead of sesame seeds. Za'atar is a Middle Eastern spice blend usually consisting of sumac, sesame seeds and thyme.

# Sponge Fingers

Also known as Lady Fingers or Savoiardi Biscuits, these light-as-air biscuits are piped, so are a good introduction to using a piping bag. Slow and steady makes perfect piping.

3 large eggs, separated
125g caster sugar, plus extra
for sprinkling
½ vanilla pod, slit lengthways and
seeds scraped out or ½ teaspoon
vanilla bean paste
pinch of salt
60g plain flour

1. **Line** two baking sheets with baking paper.

2. Tip the egg yolks into a bowl and add half of the caster sugar and all of the vanilla (seeds or paste). Using a hand-held or free-standing mixer, **whisk** on high speed until thick, pale and the mixture will hold a ribbon trail when the whisk is lifted from the bowl.

3. In another, spotlessly clean bowl whisk the egg whites with the salt until stiff but not dry. Add the remaining caster sugar in three batches, whisking well between each addition, until the egg whites are silky smooth and glossy. Using a large metal spoon, **fold** the egg whites into the yolk mixture. Sift the flour into the bowl over the mixture and fold in until thoroughly combined.

4. Fit the 1cm plain nozzle into the piping bag and then fill the piping bag with the mixture. **Pipe** even-sized lengths, roughly the size of your finger, in neat lines onto the baking paper. Keep the biscuits 2cm apart to allow enough space for them to spread during baking. Sprinkle each one with

caster sugar and leave to one side for 15 minutes while you preheat the oven to 170°C (150°C fan), Gas 3.

5. Bake the biscuits in batches on the middle shelf of the oven for about 10 minutes, until crisp and pale golden brown. Remove from the oven and leave to cool on the baking sheets.

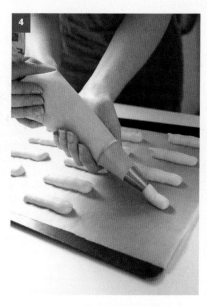

Easy does it

HANDS-ON TIME:
15 minutes,
plus 20 minutes
resting

BAKING TIME:
10 minutes

MAKES:
36 biscuits

SPECIAL
EQUIPMENT:
2 baking sheets,
large piping bag,
1cm plain nozzle

# Tuiles

Delicate tuile biscuits are ideal for serving with ice cream, sorbet or creamy desserts. You need to work fast to shape them as they harden quickly as they cool.

75g unsalted butter
2 large egg whites
pinch of salt
125g icing sugar
1 teaspoon vanilla extract
75g plain flour

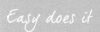

HANDS-ON TIME:
10 minutes,
plus 30 minutes
chilling

BAKING TIME:
7–8 minutes

MAKES:
24 biscuits

SPECIAL
EQUIPMENT:
2 baking sheets,
palette knife,
rolling pin

METHOD USED:
Melt and mix
method, page 24

1. Melt the butter, either in a small pan or carefully in the microwave on a low setting; cool slightly. Place the egg whites in a large bowl, add the salt and **whisk** until they will almost hold a soft, floppy peak. Add the icing sugar and whisk for a further minute until the egg whites are glossy and the sugar has been thoroughly incorporated.

2. Add the vanilla extract, Sift over the flour and gently **fold** in using a large metal spoon. Pour the cooled melted butter around the edges of the bowl and fold in until thoroughly combined. Cover and chill for 30 minutes to 1 hour.

3. Preheat the oven to 170°C (150°C fan), Gas 3 and **line** two baking sheets with baking paper.

4. Drop 4 dessertspoons of the mixture onto each tray and spread each spoonful into a thin, neat disc roughly 10–12cm in diameter with plenty of space between each tuile.

5. Bake one tray at a time on the middle shelf of the oven for about 10–12 minutes, until starting to turn golden brown at the edges. Working quickly, slide a palette knife under each tuile, lift off the tray and drape over a lightly oiled rolling pin. The tuiles harden very quickly which is why you bake only a few at a time. Repeat this baking and shaping until all of the batter has been used up. Leave to cool and finish hardening. these are best eaten on the day you bake them, but they can be **stored** in an airtight container for 2–3 days, then crisped up in a medium oven.

## Try Something Different

To make baskets for serving ice cream, use a tablespoon of mixture for each basket, spread into a slightly larger disc (15cm in diameter) and bake for 8 minutes. Working quickly, drape the hot tuiles over upturned glasses and use your hands to press each tuile into delicate folds. Leave to cool over the glass for at least 4 minutes then carefully remove and cool completely before serving. To vary the tuiles, add a teaspoon of finely grated orange or lemon zest to the batter, or scatter the tuiles with flaked almonds, pistachios or cocoa nibs halfway through baking.

# Langues de Chat

Langues de Chat, so-called because they look like a bit like a cat's tongue, are crisp wafers that are perfect for serving with ice cream, sorbets, creamy desserts or an espresso.

125g unsalted butter, at room temperature
125g icing sugar, sifted
1 teaspoon vanilla extract
finely grated zest of ½ orange
3 medium egg whites
140g plain flour
pinch of salt

1. Preheat the oven to 180°F (160°C fan), Gas 4 and **line** two baking sheets with baking paper.

2. Cream the butter with the icing sugar until pale and light, this is easiest in a free-standing mixer fitted with the creamer/paddle attachment but can be done by hand in a large bowl with a wooden spoon. Scrape down the sides of the bowl from time to time using a rubber spatula. Add the vanilla extract and orange zest and mix to combine.

3. Add the egg whites one at a time and mix again – at this point the mixture may look curdled but don't worry. Add the flour and salt and mix until thoroughly combined and the batter is smooth.

4. Fit a large piping bag with a 1cm plain nozzle. Spoon the biscuit mixture into the piping bag and **pipe** neat lines on the prepared baking sheets, 8–10cm long, leaving plenty of space between each biscuit to allow them to spread during baking. Bake in batches on the middle shelf of the oven for about 10 minutes, until the biscuits are golden brown at the edges and set in the middle. (They will crisp up further as they cool.)

5 Leave to cool on the baking sheets for 2–3 minutes and then, using a palette knife, carefully transfer to a wire rack to cool completely.

*Easy does it*

HANDS-ON TIME:
10 minutes

BAKING TIME:
10–12 minutes

MAKES:
36 small biscuits

SPECIAL EQUIPMENT:
2 baking sheets, large piping bag, 1cm plain nozzle, palette knife

METHOD USED:
Creamed method, page 25

## Try Something Different

Scatter the top of the biscuits with flaked almonds halfway through baking. **Sandwich** the biscuits with chocolate ganache (see page 145), **dip** one end of each biscuit in **melted** dark chocolate or **pipe** the tops with chocolate in zigzag lines.

# Garibaldi Biscuits

This is a slightly more indulgent version of the classic, shop-bought 'squashed fly biscuit' with a hint of nutmeg and lemon zest and plumped, juicy raisins and currants.

200g mixed raisins and currants
finely grated zest of ½ unwaxed lemon
2 tablespoons orange juice
grating of nutmeg
225g plain flour, plus extra for dusting
½ teaspoon baking powder
good pinch of salt

100g unsalted butter, chilled and diced
75g caster sugar, plus extra for sprinkling
2 medium egg yolks (save 1 white for use later)
3 tablespoons milk
1 teaspoon lemon juice
1 egg white

1. Start by preparing the filling. Tip the raisins and currants into a bowl, add the lemon zest, orange juice and nutmeg. Mix well, cover and set aside for about 2 hours, until the dried fruit has absorbed all of the liquid and become plump. You can speed up this process by popping the bowl (making sure that it is heatproof ceramic or glass) into the microwave for a minute and then stirring well. Leave until cold.

2. To make the dough, tip the flour, baking powder and salt into a large mixing bowl and mix to combine. Add the diced butter and use your fingertips to **rub** the butter into the flour. When you can no longer see or feel any butter pieces add the caster sugar and mix again until the mixture has a sandy texture.

3. Make a well in the centre, add the egg yolks, milk and lemon juice and mix using a palette knife to combine. Gather the dough into a neat ball, flatten into a disc, cover with clingfilm and chill for 1 hour until firm. **Line** two baking sheets with baking paper.

4. Lightly dust the work surface with flour and roll the dough out to a neat rectangle, 2–3mm thick. Scatter the soaked fruit in an even layer neatly over one half of the dough. **Fold** the other half of the dough over the top to completely encase the fruit. Lightly dust the rolling pin with flour and give the dough a couple of turns of the rolling pin to press the dried fruit into the dough.

5. Use a long knife to trim the edges to neaten and cut the dough into neat even rectangles, each measuring 7 × 4cm and arrange on the lined baking sheets. Chill the biscuits for 20 minutes while you preheat the oven to 180°C (160°C fan), Gas 4.

6. Prick each biscuit three times with a fork. Lightly beat the egg white and use to glaze the biscuits. Sprinkle with caster sugar. Bake in batches on the middle shelf of the oven for about 12 minutes, until crisp and golden brown, cool for a couple of minutes on the baking sheets and then transfer to a wire rack to cool completely.

*Easy does it*

HANDS-ON TIME:
15 minutes,
plus 1–2 hours chilling

BAKING TIME:
12 minutes

MAKES:
30 biscuits

SPECIAL EQUIPMENT:
2 baking sheets

METHOD USED:
Rubbed-in method, page 22

# Viennese Whirls

These delicate, melt-in-the-mouth sandwich biscuits show off your skills in piping swirls or fingers.

## For the biscuits

250g unsalted butter, softened
100g icing sugar, Sifted
1 teaspoon vanilla extract
250g plain flour
30g cornflour
½ teaspoon baking powder
pinch of salt
1 tablespoon milk

## For the buttercream filling

75g unsalted butter, at room temperature
1 teaspoon vanilla extract or
½ teaspoon vanilla bean paste
175g icing sugar, plus extra for dusting
3 tablespoons raspberry jam

HANDS-ON TIME:
15 minutes,
plus 20 minutes
chilling

BAKING TIME:
12 minutes

MAKES:
18-20 biscuits

SPECIAL
EQUIPMENT:
2 baking sheets,
large piping bag,
large star nozzle

METHOD USED:
Creamed method,
page 25

1. **Line** two baking sheets with baking paper.

2. The butter needs to be really soft, so tip it into the bowl of a free-standing mixer fitted with the creamer/paddle attachment. Cream for 2–3 minutes until pale, light and soft. Add the icing sugar and vanilla and beat again for 2–3 minutes, until smooth and soft.

3. Sift the flour, cornflour, baking powder and salt into the bowl and mix until smooth and thoroughly combined. Add the milk and mix for another 30 seconds to combine.

4. Spoon the dough into a **piping** bag fitted with a large star nozzle and pipe 10–12 tight rosette spirals, each 5cm in diameter, onto each prepared baking sheet, leaving a little space between them to allow for spreading during cooking. Chill the biscuits for 20 minutes while you preheat the oven to 170°C (150°C fan), Gas 3.

5. Bake on the middle shelf of the oven for 10–12 minutes, until pale golden at the edges. Cool on the baking sheet for 5 minutes, then use a palette knife or fish slice to carefully transfer them to a wire rack to cool completely.

6 To make the buttercream filling, beat the butter until pale and really soft, add the vanilla and mix again. Gradually add the icing sugar until the buttercream is pale, light and soft.

7 Spoon the buttercream into the clean piping bag fitted with the star nozzle. Turn half the biscuits upside down and pipe a rosette of buttercream on each. Spread the underside of the remaining biscuits with a scant teaspoon of jam and **sandwich** the halves together. Lightly dust with icing sugar to serve.

# Lemon Butter Cookies

These lemon biscuits are fresh looking and tasting. They look especially pretty when iced in contrasting colours, which makes them ideal for children's birthday parties.

### For the cookie dough

125g unsalted butter, at room temperature
125g caster sugar
finely grated zest of ½ unwaxed lemon
½ teaspoon lemon extract
1 medium egg, lightly beaten
200g plain flour, plus extra for dusting
30g cornflour
¼ teaspoon baking powder
pinch of salt

### For the icing

500g royal icing sugar
1–2 teaspoons lemon juice
food colouring pastes in assorted colours

1. Cream together the butter and caster sugar until pale and light – this is easiest and quickest using a free-standing mixer fitted with a creamer/paddle attachment or with a hand-held mixer but can also be done using the old-fashioned wooded spoon and bowl method.

2. Add the lemon zest and extract and mix well. Scrape down the sides of the bowl with a rubber spatula, add the egg and mix again until thoroughly combined.

3. In a separate bowl Sift together the flour, cornflour, baking powder and salt and gradually add to the creamed mixture. Mix until smooth and bring the dough together into a neat ball using your hands. Flatten into a disc, wrap in clingfilm and chill for 2 hours, or until firm.

4. **Line** two baking sheets with baking paper and lightly dust the work surface with flour. Roll the dough out to a thickness of about 2mm and, using the 7cm cutter, stamp out as many rounds from the dough as you can. Arrange on the prepared baking sheets and then use the smaller cutter to stamp out circles from the middle of each biscuit. Gather the dough off-cuts into a ball and re-roll to make more **shape**s. Chill the biscuits for 30 minutes and then preheat the oven to 180°C (160°C fan), Gas 4.

5. Bake on the middle shelf for about 12 minutes, until the edges of each biscuit are lightly golden and firm to the touch. Leave to cool on the baking tray for about 5 minutes before transferring to a wire rack to cool completely.
*Continued*

*Easy does it*

HANDS-ON TIME:
10 minutes,
plus 2–3 hours
chilling

BAKING TIME:
10 minutes

MAKES:
about 30 biscuits

SPECIAL
EQUIPMENT:
2 baking sheets,
7cm and 2cm round
fluted cookie cutters,
3 disposable piping
bags

METHOD USED:
Creamed method,
page 25

6. Tip the 500g royal icing sugar into a bowl and gradually add the 1–2 teaspoons of lemon juice and enough cold water to make an icing that is thick enough to coat the back of a spoon, **whisking** continuously until the icing is glossy and the right consistency. Divide the icing between three bowls and tint each a different colour using food colouring pastes. (Add the paste gradually on the point of a cocktail stick or wooden skewer until the desired shade is reached.)

7. **Dip** the top of each biscuit into icing to coat, allowing any excess to drip back into the bowl, and return the biscuits to the cooling racks. Spoon 1–2 tablespoons of each coloured icing into disposable piping bags and snip the end of each bag into a fine point.

8 **Pipe** fine lines across each biscuit in contrasting colours and then drag a clean cocktail stick or wooden skewer through the icing in opposite directions to feather. Leave until the icing has set before eating.

*Try Something Different*

Replace 30g of the flour with 30g cocoa powder and use orange zest and juice instead of lemon, or add the seeds of 1 vanilla pod instead of the lemon zest and lemon extract. Replace 30g of the plain flour with 30g finely ground pistachios and replace the lemon extract with the same amount of rosewater.

# Palmiers

Crumbly, crunchy, crisp, sugary puff pastry palmiers are a staple in most French patisseries. With only two ingredients in this recipe, the technique here is all in the shaping.

200g caster sugar
1 × 500g block all-butter puff pastry

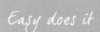

*Easy does it*

HANDS-ON TIME:
15 minutes,
plus 1 hour chilling

BAKING TIME:
20 minutes

MAKES:
about 24

SPECIAL
EQUIPMENT:
2 baking sheets

1. Liberally dust the work surface with some of the caster sugar and place the block of puff pastry on top. Dust the pastry with a coating of sugar and **roll** out to a neat 40–42cm square with a thickness of about 2mm. Turn the pastry over and around as you roll so that it is of even thickness, dusting the top and underneath with more sugar as needed to prevent the pastry from sticking to either the work surface or rolling pin.

2. Using a large knife, trim the edges to neaten and cut the pastry in half to make two neat 40 × 20cm rectangles. You will find it easier to work with two smaller pastry sections rather than one large one.

3. Scatter the work surface and the top of one pastry rectangle with more caster sugar and with one of the longer sides nearest to you, measure the long side and make a nick in the pastry to mark the middle.

*Continued*

## Try Something Different

Mix the caster sugar with either the finely grated zest of ½ unwaxed lemon or 1 tsp of ground cinnamon, then **sandwich** the cooked palmiers with a thin layer of lemon curd or chocolate and hazelnut spread. For a savoury version, replace the caster sugar with 2–3 tbsp of finely grated Parmesan mixed with a good ½ tsp of smoked paprika or 1 tsp of toasted and finely ground cumin seeds

4. Fold the outside edges in to meet in the middle and scatter the top with more caster sugar. Fold the outside edges in again to meet in the middle so that you have two neat rolls of four layers of pastry on either side of the middle. Fold the pastry rolls on top of each other as if you were closing a book. Set aside and repeat with the second pastry rectangle.

5. Wrap the rolls in clingfilm and chill in the fridge for 1 hour or the freezer for 30 minutes until firm.

6. Preheat the oven to 190°C (170°C fan), Gas 5 and **line** two baking sheets with baking paper. Lay the two rolls on top of the paper.

7. Using a sharp knife, cut the pastry rolls into slices no thicker than 1 cm and arrange, cut side uppermost, on the prepared baking sheets, leaving plenty of space between each one to allow the palmiers to spread during cooking.

8. Dust the tops of the palmiers with more caster sugar and bake on the middle shelf of the oven for 20 minutes, until golden brown and crisp.

9. Leave to cool on the baking sheets for 5 minutes and then transfer to a wire rack to cool completely.

Florentines

The fruit and nut combination in these elegant biscuits can be varied, but for a jewelled, festive look for Christmas gifts, choose a brightly coloured combination.

75g glace cherries, preferably natural coloured
75g chopped mixed candied peel
50g blanched almonds
25g shelled and unsalted slivered pistachios
25g flaked almonds
25g unsalted butter
50g demerara sugar
1 tablespoon clear honey
2 tablespoons double cream
25g plain flour
pinch of ground ginger
pinch of salt

*For the chocolate coating*
175g dark chocolate, 70 per cent cocoa solids
75g white chocolate

HANDS-ON TIME:
15 minutes,

BAKING TIME:
12 minutes

MAKES:
16 biscuits

SPECIAL EQUIPMENT:
2 baking sheets, disposable piping bag

METHOD USED:
Melt and mix method, page 24

1. Preheat the oven to 170°C (150°C fan), Gas 3 and **line** two baking sheets with baking paper.

2. Prepare the dried fruit and nuts first. Rinse the glacé cherries to remove any sticky syrup and pat dry on kitchen paper. Quarter the cherries and tip into a bowl with the candied peel. Chop the blanched almonds and add to the cherries along with the slivered pistachios and flaked almonds. Mix to combine and set aside.

Continued

*Try Something Different*

Add a nugget of finely chopped stem ginger to the mix or a handful of dried cranberries. Look out for packets of whole candied peel that you can cut into small pieces, then you can choose your favourite citrus peels and decide how large to chop the pieces.

Melt the 25g butter, 50g demerara sugar and 1 tablespoon of honey in a small pan over a low heat, stirring continuously to prevent the sugar catching on the bottom of the pan. Add the 2 tablespoons of double cream, mix to combine and pour into the bowl of fruit and nuts; mix well to combine.

Add the 25g plain flour, pinch of ground ginger and salt and mix again until smooth.

Spoon level dessertspoons of the mixture onto the prepared baking sheets, leaving plenty of space between each mound, and flatten slightly with the back of a spoon.

Bake on the middle shelf of the oven for about 12 minutes, or until the edges of the Florentines are tinged golden brown. Remove from the oven and leave to cool on the baking sheets until crisp.

7. **Melt** the 175g dark and 75g white chocolate separately in heatproof glass or ceramic bowls, either set over pans of barely simmering water. Stir until smooth, remove from the heat and leave to cool slightly. **Dip** the underside of each Florentine into the melted dark chocolate so that they have an even layer.

8. Spoon the melted white chocolate into a disposable **piping** bag, snip the end into a fine nozzle and drizzle over the dark chocolate. Leave until the chocolate has set and hardened before serving..

# Linzer Jammy Dodgers

These crumbly, nutty sandwich biscuits can be stamped into whatever shape takes your fancy – just make sure you can see the jam and they are dusted with icing sugar.

100g blanched hazelnuts
250g plain flour, plus extra for rolling out
225g unsalted butter, at room temperature
100g caster sugar
50g icing sugar
3 medium egg yolks
1 teaspoon vanilla extract
½ teaspoon baking powder
pinch of salt
4–5 tablespoons good-quality raspberry jam
icing sugar, for dusting

1. Tip the hazelnuts into a food-processor, add 1 tablespoon of the flour and whizz until finely ground. Adding the flour will prevent the nuts becoming oily as they are ground.

2. Cream together the butter, caster sugar and icing sugar until pale, light and fluffy – this will be quickest and easiest using a free-standing mixer fitted with the creamer/paddle attachment. Scrape down the sides of the mixing bowl using a rubber spatula. Add the egg yolks one at a time, mixing between each one, and then add the vanilla extract and mix again until combined.
*Continued*

*Need a little skill*

HANDS-ON TIME:
15 minutes,
plus 1 hour chilling

BAKING TIME:
10 minutes

MAKES:
about 24
sandwiched biscuits

SPECIAL
EQUIPMENT:
2 baking sheets,
6–7cm round
cookie cutter,
2cm round cookie
cutter (or use smaller
shaped cutters)

METHOD USED:
Creamed method,
page 25

## Try Something Different

Use ground almonds or pistachios instead of the hazelnuts. Replace the raspberry jam with apricot jam, or use three different types of jam for a colourful assortment of biscuits. For a chocolatey hit, **sandwich** the biscuits with chocolate and hazelnut spread or dulce de leche, or with a thin layer of chocolate bourbon buttercream – you will need about the same amount as that given on page 114.

3. Sift the remaining plain flour, baking powder and salt into the bowl. Add the ground hazelnuts and slowly mix into the creamed mixture until smooth. Flatten the dough into a disc, wrap in clingfilm and chill for 1 hour until firm. **Line** two baking sheets with baking paper.

4. On a lightly floured work surface roll half of the dough out to a thickness of 2mm. Stamp out biscuits using a 6–7cm round cookie cutter. Re-shape any leftover dough into a ball, re-roll and cut out more biscuits. Repeat with the other half of the dough.

5. Arrange the uncooked biscuits on the lined baking sheets and using smaller cutters, stamp out **shapes** from the middle of half the cookies. Chill again for 15 minutes while you preheat the oven to 170°C (150°C fan), Gas 3.

6. Bake the biscuits in batches on the middle shelf of the oven for about 12–14 minutes, or until pale golden brown. Cool on the baking sheets for 2 minutes and then carefully transfer to a cooling rack.

7. Once the biscuits are completely cold, spread a scant teaspoon of jam onto the solid biscuits leaving a 1cm border around the edge. Dust the biscuits for the top of the **sandwich** with icing sugar and press onto each jam-covered biscuit.

Chocolate
Digestives

Chocolate digestives are especially good when home-made. You can use dark or milk chocolate here or an equal mix of both – but always use 70 per cent cocoa solids dark chocolate.

175g plain wholemeal flour
100g medium oatmeal
75g plain flour, plus extra for rolling out
½ teaspoon bicarbonate of soda
pinch of salt
200g chilled unsalted butter, diced
80g soft light brown sugar
3 tablespoons milk
225g milk or dark chocolate (or a combination of both)
1 teaspoon sunflower or groundnut oil

1. Sift the wholemeal flour, oatmeal, plain flour, bicarbonate of soda and salt into a large mixing bowl. Any bran left in the sieve can be tipped back into the bowl. Add the diced butter and **rub** into the dry ingredients using your hands. You can also do this in a free-standing mixer fitted with the creamer attachment. When there are no visible flecks of butter remaining and the mixture is the texture of coarse sand, add the soft light brown sugar and mix to combine.

2. Make a well in the middle of the mixture, add the milk and use a palette knife to bring the dough together into clumps.
*Continued*

*Try Something Different*

Use wholemeal spelt flour in place of regular wholemeal flour. For a savoury version to serve with crumbly blue cheese such as Stilton, reduce the amount of sugar to 40g and omit the chocolate coating.

*Need a little skill*

HANDS-ON TIME:
10 minutes,
plus 1 hour chilling

BAKING TIME:
12 minutes

MAKES:
30 biscuits

SPECIAL EQUIPMENT:
2 baking sheets,
7cm plain round cutter

METHOD USED:
Rubbed-in method,
page 22

3. Very gently knead the dough in your hands, just to bring the dough into a neat, smooth ball. Try not to overwork the dough otherwise the resulting biscuits will be tough rather than crisp and crumbly. Flatten the dough into a disc, wrap in clingfilm and chill for 1 hour until firm.

4. **Line** two baking sheets with baking paper.

5. Lightly dust the work surface with plain flour and roll the chilled dough out to a thickness of 2–3mm. Using the cutter, stamp out as many rounds from the dough as you can and arrange on the prepared baking sheets, leaving a little space between each one. Gather any scraps and off-cuts together into a ball, re-roll and stamp out more biscuits. Prick each biscuit a couple of times with a fork and chill for 20 minutes while you preheat the oven to 170°C (150°C), Gas 3.

6. Bake the digestives on the middle shelf of the oven for about 11 minutes, until firm and light gold in colour. Cool on the trays for about 3 minutes then transfer to a wire cooling rack until cold and crisp.

7. Chop the 225g chocolate into chunks and tip into a heatproof glass or ceramic bowl. Add the 1 teaspoon of oil and place the bowl over a pan of barely simmering water to **melt**, making sure the bottom of the bowl doesn't touch the water. Stir occasionally until smooth and then remove from the heat and leave to cool slightly.

8. **Dip** the underside of each digestive biscuit into the melted chocolate, allow any excess chocolate to drip back into the bowl.

9. Place the digestive, chocolate side uppermost, either back on the wire rack or on a sheet of baking paper. Before the chocolate sets dip the flat side of the tines of a fork across each biscuit to leave ripples in the chocolate. Leave until the chocolate has set before serving or storing in an airtight container.

# Almond, Pistachio and Rosewater Biscuits

These crumbly, nutty mounds are known as Mexican Wedding Cakes or polvorones, but this recipe nods to the Middle East with rosewater, cardamom and cinnamon.

100g blanched almonds
50g pistachios (shelled and unsalted)
250g plain flour
5 green cardamom pods
125g unsalted butter, at room temperature
100g caster sugar
1–2 teaspoons rosewater
½ teaspoon ground cinnamon
pinch of salt
150g icing sugar

*Need a little skill*

HANDS-ON TIME:
20 minutes,
plus 1hour chilling

BAKING TIME:
14 minutes

MAKES:
about 30 biscuits

SPECIAL
EQUIPMENT:
2 baking sheets

METHOD USED:
Creamed method,
page 25

1. Preheat the oven to 170°C (150°C fan), Gas 3.

2. Tip the blanched almonds onto a baking sheet and toast in the oven for 4–5 minutes, until very pale golden. Watch them carefully so they don't brown too much. Leave until cold and turn the oven off for the time being.

3. Once the almonds are completely cold, tip them into a food-processor, add the pistachios and flour and whizz until finely ground. Put to one side.

4. Pound the cardamom pods using a pestle and mortar to release the small black seeds from the husks. Discard the husks and continue to pound the seeds until finely ground.

5. Cream the butter with the caster sugar until soft, pale and light – this is easiest and quickest using a free-standing mixer fitted with a creamer/paddle attachment. Scrape down the sides of the bowl with a rubber spatula from time to time. Add the rosewater and mix again.

6. Sift the remaining flour, cinnamon salt into the bowl, add the ground nuts and crushed cardamom seeds and mix again until thoroughly combined. Scoop the dough into a clean bowl, cover with clingfilm and chill for 1–2 hours.

7. Preheat the oven to 170°C (150°C fan), Gas 3 and **line** two baking sheets with baking paper. Tip the 150g icing sugar into a large, shallow bowl.

8. Using a dessertspoon and your hands, scoop up walnut-sized nuggets of dough and roll into balls. Arrange on the lined baking sheets, leaving a little space between each one to allow for spreading, and bake on the middle shelf of the oven for about 12–14 minutes, until firm and pale golden brown.

9. Leave the biscuits to cool on the baking sheets for 10 minutes and then toss them in the icing sugar to coat. Transfer to a wire rack and leave until cold before dusting with more icing sugar to serve.

# Stained Glass Biscuits

These cookies look beautiful hanging at a window, the light shining through the 'stained glass'. Try to fill the holes neatly so you don't scatter sweets over the dough or overfill the holes.

225g unsalted butter, softened
150g icing sugar
1 medium egg, beaten
1 egg yolk
1 teaspoon vanilla extract
350g plain flour, plus extra for rolling out

1 teaspoon ground ginger
1 teaspoon ground cinnamon
pinch of salt
1 tablespoon milk, if needed
200g boiled sweets in assorted flavours and colours

1 Using a free-standing mixer fitted with the creamer/paddle attachment, cream together the softened butter and icing sugar until pale and light, scraping down the sides of the bowl from time to time with a rubber spatula. You can also use an electric hand-held whisk or a wooden spoon and plenty of muscle power. Add the whole egg and egg yolk and vanilla extract and mix again until thoroughly combined.
*Continued*

HANDS-ON TIME:
12 minutes,
plus 1–2 hours
chilling

BAKING TIME:
12 minutes

MAKES:
24 biscuits

SPECIAL
EQUIPMENT:
snowflake or star-
shaped cutters in
assorted sizes, 2
baking sheets

METHOD USED:
Creamed method,
page 25

2 Sift the 350g plain flour with the 1 teaspoon of ground ginger and 1 teaspoon of ground cinnamon and a pinch of salt into the bowl and mix again adding a drop of milk if needed to make the dough come together smoothly.

3 Gather the dough into a ball, flatten into a disc and wrap in clingfilm. Chill for a couple of hours, or until firm.

4 Meanwhile, divide the 200g boiled sweets into separate colours, and crush each colour separately into small pieces in a pestle and mortar. Wash the pestle and mortar between each colour. Alternatively, you could just place each colour in a double thickness of freezer bags, and crush them using a rolling pin.

5 Preheat the oven to 180°C (160°C fan), 350°F, Gas 4 and **line** two baking sheets with baking paper.

6 Lightly dust the work surface with plain flour and roll out the dough until it is 3mm thick. Using the snowflake or star-shaped cookie cutters, stamp out **shapes** in assorted sizes and arrange on the prepared baking sheets. Stamp out and remove smaller shapes from the middle of each biscuit, leaving a neat hole in the middle. Carefully and neatly fill the holes in the snowflakes with one colour of the crushed boiled sweets, filling them just shallower than the depth of the biscuits. Bake in batches on the middle shelf of the preheated oven for about 12 minutes, until the cookies are pale golden and the boiled sweets have melted and filled the holes.

7 Gather any dough scraps into a neat ball, re-roll and shape more biscuits and fill and bake as before. Leave the biscuits to cool on the baking sheets until they are firm and the 'stained glass' centres have hardened.

Custard
Creams

These old school favourites have a few added extras that you won't find in shop-bought packs – a double hit of custard powder in the biscuit dough and also in the buttercream.

225g plain flour, plus extra for rolling out
½ teaspoon baking powder
50g custard powder
50g icing sugar
pinch of salt
175g unsalted butter, chilled and diced
1 tablespoon milk
1 teaspoon vanilla extract

### For the filling
50g white chocolate, chopped
100g unsalted butter, softened
50g icing sugar
1 tablespoon custard powder
1 teaspoon vanilla extract

1. Sift the flour, baking powder, custard powder, icing sugar and salt into the bowl of a food-processor and whizz for 30 seconds to combine. Add the diced butter and process until it has been completely rubbed into the dry ingredients. You can also do this step using a free-standing mixer fitted with a creamer/paddle attachment or **rub** the butter into the dry ingredients using your hands.

2. Add the milk and vanilla extract and mix again just until the dough starts to clump together. Tip the dough into a large mixing bowl and use your hands to squeeze and very lightly knead the dough into a smooth ball but don't overwork the mixture or your resulting cookies will shrink and toughen as they bake. Flatten into a disc, cover with cling film and chill for 1 hour.

3. Preheat the oven to 180°C (160°C fan), Gas 4 and **line** two baking sheets with baking paper.
*Continued*

*Continued*

### Try Something Different

These biscuits can be made with various flavours. Add desiccated coconut to the custard, or a few drops of lemon juice, or cocoa powder.

## Need a little skill

HANDS-ON TIME:
15 minutes,
plus 1 hour chilling

BAKING TIME:
10 minutes

MAKES:
20 biscuits

SPECIAL EQUIPMENT:
2 baking sheets,
5cm square
cookie cutters

METHOD USED:
Rubbed-in method,
page 24

4. Lightly dust the work surface with plain flour and roll out the dough to a thickness of 2mm. Using cookie cutters, stamp out **shapes** and arrange on the lined baking sheets. Gather any scraps of dough together and shape into a smooth-ish ball, then re-roll and stamp out more cookies. Press decorative indent patterns into the top of each cookie (one trick is to use the lemon zesting side of a box grater) and bake on the middle shelf of the oven for about 10–11 minutes, or until firm and starting to turn very pale golden at the edges.

5. Remove from the oven and leave the biscuits to rest on the baking sheet for few minutes and then transfer to a wire rack to cool completely.

6. Meanwhile prepare the custard filling. **Melt** the 50g white chocolate in a small heatproof bowl, over a pan of barely simmering water. (Make sure the bottom of the bowl doesn't touch the water.) Remove from the heat, stir until smooth and leave to cool. Beat the 100g butter, 50g icing sugar, 1 tablespoon of custard powder and 1 teaspoon of vanilla extract together until smooth, pale and light. Add the cooled, melted white chocolate and stir until smooth.

7. Use a palette knife to spread the underside of half of the cookies with buttercream and **sandwich** with the remaining cookies, making sure that they are pretty-side outermost.

Malted Milk
Sandwich
Biscuits

Malty, sweet, light and crisp, these biscuits can either be filled with a rich chocolate buttercream or eaten singly and simply, just coated in a melted chocolate glaze.

### For the biscuits

150g unsalted butter, at room temperature
100g caster sugar
1 teaspoon vanilla extract or vanilla bean paste
1 medium egg
1 medium egg yolk
250g plain flour
75g malted milk powder
½ teaspoon baking powder
pinch of salt

### For the malted chocolate buttercream

75g dark chocolate, preferably a minimum of 70 per cent cocoa solids
75g unsalted butter, at room temperature
50g icing sugar, sifted
2 tablespoons malted milk powder
1 tablespoon milk

HANDS-ON TIME:
10 minutes,
plus1 hour chilling

BAKING TIME:
11 minutes

MAKES:
about 24
sandwiched
biscuits

SPECIAL
EQUIPMENT:
2 baking sheets,
5–6cm round cutter

METHOD USED:
Creamed method,
page 25

1. Cream the softened butter and caster sugar until pale and light – this is easiest using a free-standing mixer fitted with the creamer/paddle attachment. Scrape down the sides of the bowl from time to time using a rubber spatula. Add the vanilla and mix again to combine.

2. In a small bowl lightly beat the egg and egg yolk together and gradually add to the creamed butter mixture, mixing well between each addition and scraping down the sides of the mixing bowl. Sift the plain flour, malted milk powder, baking powder and salt directly into the bowl and mix again until smooth and thoroughly combined. Do not over-mix the dough as this will result in tough rather than crisp cookies. Gather the dough into a ball, flatten into a disc and wrap in clingfilm. Chill for 1 hour until firm.

3. Preheat the oven to 170°C (150°C fan), Gas 3 and **line** two baking sheets with baking paper.

4. Lightly dust the work surface with plain flour and roll the dough out to a thickness of 2mm. Stamp out biscuits using the plain round cutter.
*Continued*

### Try Something Different

Omit the buttercream filling and instead **dip** one side of each biscuit in **melted** milk or dark chocolate.

Arrange the biscuits on the prepared baking sheets leaving a little space between each one. If you like, gently press the top (thicker) side of a smaller cutter into the discs to make a rim, and use the end of the skewer to indent little button holes in the centre.

Bake in batches on the middle shelf of the oven for about 11 minutes, until firm and golden at the edges. (Swap the baking sheets around halfway through baking to ensure that they bake evenly.)

Leave to cool on the trays for a few minutes before transferring to wire racks to cool completely.

Meanwhile prepare the malted chocolate buttercream. Break the 75g chocolate into chunks and place in a heatproof ceramic or glass bowl. Set the bowl over a pan of barely simmering water (make sure the bottom of the bowl does not touch the water) to **melt** the chocolate. Stir until smooth, remove from the heat and leave to

cool slightly. Tip the 75g butter into a bowl and beat until soft and light, either using a free-standing mixer, hand-held electric whisk or with a wooden spoon. Gradually add the 50g sifted icing sugar, one tablespoon at a time, and mix until really pale and light.

8. In another small bowl mix the 2 tablespoons of malted milk powder with the 1 tablespoon of milk to a smooth paste. Add to the creamed butter and icing sugar along with the melted, cooled chocolate. Beat until smooth and thoroughly combined.

9. Turn half of the malted milk biscuits upside down and top with a teaspoon of the malted chocolate buttercream. **Sandwich** with a naked biscuit and press gently together. Leave until set firm before serving.

# Chocolate Bourbon Creams

Two rich, crisp chocolate biscuits sandwiched together with a layer of decadent chocolate buttercream – these are the biscuits of fond teatime childhood memories.

## For the biscuits

125g unsalted butter, at room temperature
100g caster sugar, plus extra for sprinkling
1 tablespoon golden syrup
½ teaspoon vanilla extract
1 large egg yolk
225g plain flour, plus extra for dusting
30g cocoa powder
½ teaspoon bicarbonate of soda
pinch of salt
1 tablespoon milk

## For the chocolate buttercream

150g unsalted butter, at room temperature
225g icing sugar
75g cocoa powder
1–2 tablespoons milk

1. Cream the softened butter and caster sugar until pale and light – this is easiest and quickest using a free-standing mixer fitted with a creamer/paddle attachment. Scrape down the sides of the bowl from time to time using a rubber spatula. Add the golden syrup, vanilla extract and egg yolk and mix again until smooth and thoroughly combined.

2. Sift the flour, cocoa powder, bicarbonate of soda and salt into the bowl. Add the milk and mix again until the dough is smooth. Shape into a ball, flatten into a disc and wrap in clingfilm. Chill for 1 hour to firm up.
*Continued*

## Try Something Different

For a white chocolate filling simply replace the cocoa powder with **melted** and cooled white chocolate and replace the milk with 1 teaspoon of vanilla extract.

Need a little skill

HANDS-ON TIME:
10 minutes,
plus 1 hour chilling

BAKING TIME:
12 minutes

MAKES:
about 24
sandwiched
biscuits

SPECIAL
EQUIPMENT:
2 baking sheets
Bourbon biscuit
cutter (optional)

METHOD USED:
Creamed method,
page 25

3. Cover two baking sheets with baking paper. Lightly dust the work surface with plain flour and roll out the chilled dough to a neat rectangle with a thickness of 2mm. Using a ruler as a guide, cut the dough into neat 4 x 8cm rectangles, or use a rectangular cutter. Arrange on the prepared baking sheets, leaving a little space between each biscuit. Gather the dough off-cuts into a ball and re-roll to make more shapes.

4. Prick with a fork or stamp bourbon lettering across each biscuit and chill again for 15 minutes while you preheat the oven to 180°C (160°C fan), Gas 4.

5. Sprinkle the biscuits with caster sugar and bake in batches on the middle shelf of the oven for 10–12 minutes, until firm and crisp. Cool the bourbons on the baking sheet for a few minutes and then carefully transfer to a wire rack to cool completely.

6. Meanwhile prepare the chocolate buttercream filling. Beat the 150g butter in a bowl with a wooden spoon until soft and light. Sift the 225g icing sugar and 75g cocoa powder into a bowl and gradually add to the creamed butter, mixing well between each addition until smooth. Add the 1–2 tablespoons of milk, a little at a time, until the buttercream is a good spreading consistency.

7. Turn half of the bourbon biscuits upside down and spread with a teaspoon of the buttercream. Top with another biscuit gently pressing the two together.

Biscotti

Serve these crisp Italian cookies alongside a creamy dessert for a crunchy contrast, or eat after dinner alongside an espresso or dunked into a glass of vin santo.

100g whole almonds
275g plain flour
150g caster sugar
½ teaspoon baking powder
1 teaspoon anise seeds
pinch of salt
finely grated zest of ½ orange
finely grated zest of ½ lemon
2 large eggs
1 tablespoon Marsala or orange juice
1 teaspoon vanilla extract

*Need a little skill*

HANDS-ON TIME:
10 minutes,

BAKING TIME:
1 hour

MAKES:
about 30 biscuits

SPECIAL EQUIPMENT:
2 baking sheets

1. Preheat the oven to 170°C (150°C fan), Gas 3 and **line** a large baking sheet with baking paper.

2. Roughly chop the almonds and tip into a large mixing bowl with the plain flour, caster sugar, baking powder, anise seeds and salt. Add the orange and lemon zests and mix well to thoroughly combine. Make a well in the centre.

3. **Beat** together the eggs, Marsala or orange juice and vanilla extract in a separate bowl. Pour into the well in the centre of the dry ingredients and mix until thoroughly combined and the dough comes together into a smooth ball. You will find this easiest initially using a wooden spoon or rubber spatula but then switch to your hands to bring the dough into a smooth ball. *Continued.*

## Try Something Different

Make a chocolate and pistachio version. Follow the recipe above, using the following ingredients: 75g shelled and unsalted pistachios, 230g plain flour, 175g caster sugar, 40g cocoa powder, ½ tsp baking powder, pinch of salt, 75g dark chocolate chips, 1 tsp finely grated orange zest, 2 large eggs, 1 large egg yolk, 1 tbsp Marsala or orange juice and 1 tsp vanilla extract. **Dip** half of each biscotti in either white or dark **melted** chocolate. Add a handful of either dried sour cherries or cranberries to the dough along with the nuts.

4 Lightly dust your hands with plain flour and divide the dough into two even pieces. Roll out each piece into a log roughly 20cm long and 4–5cm in diameter. Arrange on the prepared baking sheet, placing the logs well apart to allow for spreading during baking.

5 Cook on the middle shelf of the oven for 20–25 minutes, or until light golden in colour, turning the tray around after 10–15 minutes to ensure that the logs brown evenly. Remove from the oven and leave to cool for 30–45 minutes, turn the oven down to 150°C (130°C fan), Gas 2 and line another baking sheet with a clean piece of baking paper.

6 Using a long serrated or bread knife, cut the cooled biscotti logs on the diagonal into slices, each about 5mm thick. Lay the slices in a single layer on the prepared baking sheets and return to the oven for a further 10 minutes, until pale golden brown and crisp.

Turn the biscotti over and swap the baking sheets around halfway through the baking time to ensure that they crisp evenly. Transfer to a wire rack to cool and keep in an airtight container until required.

# Millionaire's Shortbread

These indulgent squares have something for everyone: a crisp, buttery shortbread base, topped with luscious, slightly salted caramel and a thin layer of dark chocolate.

## For the shortbread
125g plain flour
pinch of salt
125g unsalted butter, chilled and diced
50g icing sugar

## For the caramel
125g caster sugar
75g golden syrup
50g light muscovado sugar
250ml double cream
½ teaspoon vanilla bean paste
75g unsalted butter
a pinch of sea salt flakes
25g dark chocolate, finely chopped

## For the topping
125g dark chocolate, preferably a minimum of 70 per cent cocoa solids
50g white chocolate

HANDS-ON TIME:
20 minutes,
plus 2 hours chilling

BAKING TIME:
15 minutes

MAKES:
16 squares

SPECIAL EQUIPMENT:
20cm square baking tin

METHOD USED:
Rubbed-in method,
page 22

1. Preheat the oven to 180°C (160°C fan), Gas 4 and **line** the base and sides of the baking tin with baking paper.

2. Start by making the shortbread base. Tip the flour and salt into either a large mixing bowl or the bowl of a food-processor. Add the diced butter and **rub** into the flour, either using your fingertips or the pulse button on the food-processor. When there are no visible specks of butter remaining add the icing sugar and mix again to combine. Continue pulsing or rubbing in until the dough just starts to clump together.

3. Tip the shortbread mix into the prepared tin and press level using your fingertips or the back of a spoon.
Continued

Bake on the middle shelf of the oven for 12–14 minutes, or until golden brown. Remove from the oven and leave to cool.

To make the caramel, tip the 125g caster sugar, 75g golden syrup and 50g light muscovado sugar into a medium sized saucepan. Add the 250ml double cream, ½ teaspoon vanilla bean paste and 75g unsalted butter. Set the pan over a low heat and, stirring frequently, melt the butter and dissolve the sugar.

When the mixture is smooth, pop a sugar thermometer into the pan and raise the heat slightly to bring the caramel to the boil. Continue cooking at a steady but not furious pace, stirring from time to time to prevent the caramel scorching on the bottom of the pan. When the caramel reaches 120°C or just over the soft ball stage, slide the pan off the heat. If you don't have a sugar thermometer you can test the caramel by dropping a ½ teaspoonful of the caramel into a cup of very cold water – it should set into a firm but not hardball.

Remove the thermometer from the pan and when the bubbling subsides add the chopped chocolate and a good pinch of sea salt flakes. Stir to

combine and pour the caramel into the tin over the baked shortbread. The caramel should cover the shortbread in a smooth layer. Leave until completely cold and set firm.

8 Finely chop the 125g dark chocolate for the topping and tip into a heatproof glass or ceramic bowl. Set over a pan of barely simmering water – do not allow the bottom of the bowl to touch the water or you could scorch the chocolate. Stir until smooth and completely **melted**, then remove from the heat and leave to cool for about 10 minutes.

9 Pour over the top of the caramel and spread the chocolate in an even layer using an offset palette knife; leave until set firm. Melt the 50g white chocolate in the same way, stirring until smooth. Remove from the heat and leave to cool slightly before spooning it into a disposable piping bag. Snip the end into a fine point and **pipe** lines of white chocolate over the dark chocolate and drag the point of a cocktail stick or wooden skewer through the lines to make a delicate feathered pattern in the chocolate. Leave until set before cutting into squares to serve.

# Brandy Snaps

Success in making these delicate brandy snaps is down to timing; you need to work quickly to shape them while pliable, but when cool enough to handle. Practice makes perfect.

sunflower oil, for greasing
125g unsalted butter
125g caster sugar
125g (4 level tablespoons) golden syrup
pinch of salt
125g plain flour
1 teaspoon ground ginger
1 tablespoon lemon juice

1. Preheat the oven to 190°C (170°C fan), Gas 5 and **line** two or three baking sheets with baking paper. Using kitchen paper, lightly grease the handles of four wooden spoons with a little sunflower oil.

2. Place the butter, caster sugar, golden syrup and salt into a small, heavy-based pan. You'll find it easier to measure the golden syrup if you heat the measuring spoon in a mug of boiling hot water for a minute or so beforehand. Heat the mixture gently, stirring from time to time until it is smooth and the butter has melted and the sugar completely dissolved. Remove from the heat and leave to cool for 1 minute.

3. Sift the flour and ground ginger together into the pan with the lemon juice. Beat with a wooden spoon until smooth and then leave to rest for a further 2 minutes.

*Continued*

*Continued*

## Try Something Different

For a more indulgent treat fill the cooled brandy snaps. Whip 300ml double cream to soft peaks with either ½ tsp vanilla bean paste or the finely grated zest of ½ orange, one tablespoon of brandy and a pinch of ground cinnamon. Spoon into a **piping** bag fitted with a large star nozzle and pipe the cream into each end of the brandy snaps. Serve immediately.

*Need a little skill*

HANDS-ON TIME:
10 minutes

BAKING TIME:
9 minutes

MAKES:
about 20 biscuits

SPECIAL EQUIPMENT:
2–3 baking sheets, 4 wooden spoons

METHOD USED:
Melt and mix method, page 24

4 Spoon level dessertspoons of the mixture onto the prepared baking sheets, spacing each mound well apart and with no more than four brandy snaps on each sheet as they will spread during baking. You will also find it hard to juggle shaping more than four brandy snaps at a time.

5 Bake in batches on the middle shelf of the oven for 8–9 minutes, until the brandy snaps are thin, lacy in texture and a light amber colour. Remove from the oven and leave to cool for about 20–30 seconds to firm up slightly.

6 Working quickly, slide a palette knife under one brandy snap and carefully drape one end of the biscuit over the handle of a wooden spoon with the top of the biscuit uppermost. Turn the handle of the spoon around so that the

brandy snap forms a neat tube with the spoon handle inside – use your other hand to gently press the biscuit into shape. Rest the spoon over an empty bowl to allow the brandy snap to cool and harden.

7. Repeat with the remaining baked biscuits. Cool for about 3 minutes and then carefully slide the brandy snaps off the wooden spoons and onto a wire rack. If you leave the biscuits on the spoons for too long you may find that they are too crisp and will be tricky to remove from the spoons without breaking.

8. Repeat the baking and shaping until all the mixture is used up. **Store** in layers between sheets of baking paper in an airtight container for up to 3 days

Jaffa Cakes

These biscuits (or are they cakes?) are elevated to lofty heights when home-made with the best ingredients.

## For the orange jelly

3 leaves platinum-grade leaf gelatine
225ml freshly squeezed orange juice
150g shredless orange marmalade

## For the chocolate layer

200g dark chocolate, preferably a minimum of 70 per cent cocoa solids, chopped
1 teaspoon sunflower or groundnut oil, plus extra for greasing

## For the cake bases

100g unsalted butter, at room temperature, plus extra for greasing
75g caster sugar
1 medium egg
1 medium egg yolk
½ teaspoon vanilla extract
60g plain flour
¼ teaspoon baking powder
40g ground almonds
pinch of salt
2 teaspoons milk

### Need a little skill

HANDS-ON TIME:
2 hours,
plus overnight
setting

BAKING TIME:
12 minutes

MAKES:
20–24 biscuits

SPECIAL
EQUIPMENT:
20 × 30cm
baking tin,
2 × 12-hole
muffin tins,
4–5cm plain
round cutter,
palette knife

METHOD USED:
Creamed method,
page 25

1. Prepare the orange jelly first. Lightly grease the 20 × 30cm baking tin with oil and **line** the base and sides with a piece of clingfilm. Soak the 3 gelatine leaves in a bowl of cold water for 10 minutes, until soft and floppy.

2. Pour the orange juice and marmalade into a small pan and heat gently to melt the marmalade. Bring to the boil and then remove from the heat. Lift the softened gelatine leaves from the cold water, blot briefly on kitchen paper or a clean tea towel to remove any excess water and add to the hot orange juice. **Whisk** to melt and then pour into the clingfilm-lined baking tin. Leave until cool and then chill for at least 4 hours or preferably overnight until set firm.

3. Preheat the oven to 170°C (150°C fan), Gas 3 and grease the holes of the muffin tins with a little butter. Line the base of each muffin cup with a small disc of buttered baking paper.

*Continued*

Cream the 100g butter with the 75g caster sugar until light and fluffy. Gradually add the 1 egg and 1 egg yolk, a little at a time, scraping down the sides of the bowl with a rubber spatula between additions. Add the ½ teaspoon of vanilla extract and mix again. Sift the 60g flour, ¼ teaspoon of baking powder, 40g ground almonds and a pinch of salt into the bowl. Add the 2 teaspoons of milk and mix again until smooth.

Divide the mixture between the prepared muffin tins – each muffin cup should have just over 1 teaspoon of mixture; you should have enough batter to make 20 cakes. Spread level with either an offset palette knife or the back of a teaspoon and bake on the middle shelf of the oven for about 12 minutes, until pale golden at the edges.

Run a palette knife around the edge of each cake to release it and turn out onto a wire rack. Peel off the baking

paper circles, turn the cakes the right side up and leave to cool completely.

7. Using the clingfilm to help you, carefully lift the orange jelly from the tray and onto a board. Using the 4–5cm cutter, stamp out circles from the jelly. Carefully lift the jelly circles off the clingfilm using a palette knife and place on top of each sponge base.

8. Chop the 200g chocolate, tip into a heatproof bowl and add the 1 teaspoon of sunflower oil. **Melt** the chocolate by placing the bowl over a pan of barely simmer water, making sure the bottom of the bowl doesn't touch the water. Stir until smooth, remove from the heat and leave to cool for a few minutes. Carefully spoon melted chocolate over each jelly-topped cake, allowing it to completely cover the jelly and any exposed sponge. Press the tines of a fork into the chocolate to make decorative ridges and leave in a cool place until the chocolate has set firm.

Lemony
Spiced
and Iced
Biscuits

Let your imagination run wild, and shape these as numbers and letters or fancy dancing shoes and Fabergé eggs.

225g unsalted butter, softened
150g icing sugar
1 medium egg, lightly beaten
grated zest of ½ unwaxed lemon
1 teaspoon vanilla bean paste
350g plain flour, plus extra for rolling out
pinch of salt

*For the icing*
500g royal icing sugar
75–100ml water
pink and blue food colouring pastes

*Up for a challenge*

HANDS-ON TIME:
30 minutes,
plus chilling and
decorating

BAKING TIME:
12 minutes

MAKES:
about 20 biscuits,
depending on
cutters used

SPECIAL
EQUIPMENT:
baking sheets,
large number cutters,
disposable piping
bags

METHOD USED:
Creamed method,
page 25

1 In a large bowl cream the softened butter and icing sugar until pale, light and fluffy. This will be easiest and quickest using a free-standing mixer fitted with a creamer/paddle attachment but can also be done by hand with a wooden spoon. Scrape down the sides of the bowl with a rubber spatula and gradually add the beaten egg, mixing well until smooth. Add the lemon zest and vanilla bean paste and mix again.

2 Sift the plain flour and salt into the bowl and mix until smooth. Shape the mixture into a disc, wrap in clingfilm and chill for a couple of hours or until firm. **Line** two baking sheets with baking paper.

3 Lightly dust the work surface with plain flour and roll the cookie dough out to a thickness of 2–3mm. Using the number cookie cutters, stamp out biscuits and arrange on the prepared baking sheets. Gather any off-cuts, re-roll and stamp out more biscuits. Chill for 20 minutes while you preheat the oven to 180°C (160°C fan), 350°F, Gas 4.

4 Bake the biscuits in batches on the middle shelf of the oven for 10–12 minutes, or until pale golden. Remove from the oven and cool on the baking sheets until firm before carefully transferring to a wire rack to cool completely.

*Continued*

5 Sift the 500g royal icing sugar into a bowl and gradually add the 75–100ml water – you want just enough to make a smooth, spreadable icing. Beat or **whisk** until smooth and lump-free. The icing should be thick enough to hold a firm ribbon trail when the spoon or whisk is lifted from the bowl.

6 Divide the icing between 3 separate bowls. Leave one bowl of icing white and cover with clingfilm until ready to use. Using a wooden skewer or cocktail stick add pink food colouring paste in small increments to one bowl and mix well until the desired shade is reached. Always add the colour a little at a time,

mixing well between each addition, it's easier to add more colouring to build up the depth of colour and impossible to take it away if you've been a little too enthusiastic! Cover and set aside. In the same way add blue food colouring to the third bowl of icing, cover and set aside.

7 Now you can fill your **piping** bag. Spoon 2–3 tablespoons of the white icing into a piping bag and squeeze or press the icing towards the nozzle end. Twist the open top to seal and prevent any icing escaping all over your hands then use sharp scissors to snip the nozzle end into a fine point. Taking

one biscuit at a time, and with a steady hand, pipe a fine, continuous line of white icing around the top outside edge of the biscuit and another round the inside edge of each shape – this inside line only applies to numbers that have a hole in the middle such as 4, 6, 8 and 9. This will create a section in the middle of the biscuit that will later be flooded with coloured icing. Repeat with all of the biscuits and then leave the icing to dry for 30 minutes.

8 Divide the biscuits in half – half will be iced pink and the other half with the blue icing. Add a drop more water to the reserved pink icing to make it just slightly runnier than the piping icing – about the consistency of double cream – and use a teaspoon to spoon the icing into the middle of the outline that you have previously piped. Using a small palette knife, carefully spread the icing in a smooth layer to fill the outline. Leave to dry for about 2 minutes and then pipe white polka dots all over the pink icing. Repeat this icing and dotting until all of the biscuits are fully decorated in either pink or blue icing.

9 Leave for at least 1 hour for the icing to dry and set firm before serving.

# Mochaccino Macarons

Mastering macarons is not as tricky as you'd think – the skill is in piping the mixture into neat and even circles. Eat them the day after they are made for the best flavour and chewy texture.

### For the macaron shells
175g ground almonds
175g icing sugar
150g egg whites (about 4 medium egg whites – keep 2 yolks for use later)
pinch of salt
200g caster sugar
2 teaspoons instant espresso powder/granules
½ teaspoon brown food colouring paste

### For the mocha cream filling
100g dark chocolate, preferably a minimum of 70 percent cocoa solids, chopped
2 large egg yolks
50g caster sugar
½ teaspoon instant espresso powder/granules
150g unsalted butter, at room temperature

*Up for a challenge*

HANDS-ON TIME:
20 minutes, plus 30 minutes resting

BAKING TIME:
12–13 minutes

MAKES:
about 30 biscuits

SPECIAL EQUIPMENT:
4cm plain round cookie cutter, 2 baking sheets, large piping bag, 1cm plain round piping nozzle

1. Take two sheets of baking paper and, using the cookie cutter as a guide, draw around the cutter to make 30 evenly spaced, 4cm circles on each piece of baking paper. Try to keep the circles in neat lines, leaving a little space between each. Turn the paper over so that the pencil lines are now on the underside – you should be able to see them through the paper – and place one piece on each baking sheet. Fit the large piping bag with the 1cm round nozzle, twist the bag just above the nozzle and sit the bag in a jug so that the top is folded back and open wide.

2. Tip the ground almonds and icing sugar into a food-processor and blitz for 30 seconds to 1 minute to thoroughly mix. Add 70g of the egg whites and pulse again until combined into a smooth, thick paste.

3. Tip the remaining egg whites and a pinch of salt into a medium-large heatproof glass or ceramic mixing bowl and add the caster sugar. Dissolve the coffee in 1 tablespoon of boiling water, add to the egg whites and set the bowl over a pan of simmering water. Be sure that the bottom of the bowl does not come into contact with the water or you will scramble the egg whites. Beat constantly with a balloon whisk or electric hand whisk for 3–4 minutes until the sugar has completely dissolved and the egg whites are glossy white, silky smooth, thickened enough to hold a ribbon trail and are hot to the touch.

4. Quickly scoop the meringue mixture into the bowl of a free-standing mixer, add the brown food colouring and **whisk** over a medium-high heat for a further 3 minutes, until the meringue is glossy and has cooled and thickened enough to hold a firm ribbon trail when the whisk is lifted from the bowl. *Continued*

139

5. Using a rubber spatula, scoop the almond mixture from the food-processor into a bowl (use the one that you used for the bain-marie to save on washing up) and add one quarter of the meringue. **Fold** in using a rubber spatula or large metal spoon to loosen the almond paste. Add this back to the meringue and fold in using large strokes, continuing to mix until thoroughly combined and the mixture resembles thick molten lava that will hold a ribbon trail for about 5 seconds.

6. Working quickly, scoop the mixture into the prepared piping bag and **pipe** 30 even sized macarons onto each baking paper-lined sheet, using the circles as a guide. Sharply bang the baking sheets on the work surface to pop any air bubbles and set aside for about 30 minutes, until a light skin has formed on the surface of each macaron shell. Preheat the oven to 170°C (150°C fan), Gas 3.

7. Bake the macarons, one tray at a time, on the middle shelf of the oven for 12–13 minutes until well risen and crisp with well-defined 'feet'.

8. Remove from the oven and leave to cool completely on the trays while you prepare the mocha cream filling. **Melt** the 100g chocolate in a heatproof bowl over a pan of barely simmering water. Stir until smooth and leave to cool slightly.

9. Place the 2 egg yolks in a medium heatproof glass or ceramic bowl and set aside. Tip the 50g caster sugar into a small pan, add 3 tablespoons of water and set over a low heat to dissolve the sugar. Bring to the boil and simmer for 30 seconds to thicken slightly. Dissolve the ½ teaspoon of instant espresso in 1 teaspoon of boiling water, add to the syrup and pour over the egg yolks, whisking continuously until smooth. Set the bowl over a pan of simmering water and continue to whisk for a further 2–3 minutes until pale and thickened. Remove from the heat and whisk for a further 2–3 minutes until cool.

10. Gradually add the 150g butter, a little at a time and whisking between each addition until smooth. Add the melted chocolate, fold in and leave for 30 minutes to firm up slightly.

11. To assemble the macarons: turn half of the shells over so that they are flat side uppermost and top with a teaspoon of mocha cream. Top with another shell, pressing them gently together so that the cream is visible from the sides. Stack the macarons in a tray, cover with clingfilm and chill overnight before serving.

Cigarettes
Russes

Practice make perfect for these delicate biscuits. The technique needed for rolling these wafers is similar to that used in brandy snaps – just on a finer scale, using a straw.

Up for a challenge

## For the biscuits

75g unsalted butter
4 large egg whites
pinch of salt
150g icing sugar, sifted
1 teaspoon vanilla extract
100g plain flour
1 teaspoon cocoa powder

## For the ganache filling

100g dark chocolate, preferably a minimum of 70 per cent cocoa solids, finely chopped
100ml double cream
1 tablespoon light muscovado sugar
drop of vanilla extract
pinch of salt

## For the decoration

75g white chocolate
75g dark chocolate, preferably a minimum of 70 per cent cocoa solids
2 tablespoons very finely chopped toasted hazelnuts
2 tablespoons finely chopped blanched pistachios

HANDS-ON TIME:
10 minutes,
plus overnight
resting

BAKING TIME:
3–4 minutes per
baking sheet but
1 hour in total

MAKES:
20–24 biscuits

SPECIAL
EQUIPMENT:
plastic ice cream
tub lid,
several baking sheets,
silicone baking
mats (optional),
disposable piping
bags,
offset palette knife,
6 drinking straws

1. For best results you will need to make the mixture for these biscuits at least 2 hours (but preferably the day before) you plan to start baking.

2. Melt the butter, either in a small pan over a low heat or in a heatproof bowl in short bursts in the microwave. Set aside to cool slightly.

3. Tip the 4 egg whites and a pinch of salt into a large mixing bowl and beat with a balloon whisk until just foamy. Add the 150g sifted icing sugar and 1 teaspoon of vanilla extract and **whisk** again until smooth. Sift the 100g plain flour into the bowl and beat until combined. Pour the melted butter around the inside edge of the bowl and whisk until the batter is smooth.

4. Spoon 100g of the batter into a small bowl, add the 1 teaspoon of cocoa powder and mix to combine. Cover both bowls with clingfilm and chill for at least 2 hours but preferably overnight.
*Continued*

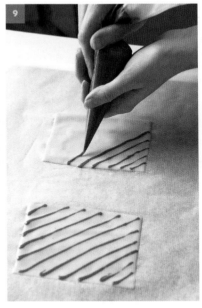

5. While the batter is resting prepare the plastic template. Take your ice cream tub lid and with the help of a ruler draw an 8 x 12cm rectangle in the middle. Using a craft knife or sharp scissors, cut out the rectangle, leaving a neat hole in the middle of the plastic. This will be your template.

6. Preheat the oven to 180°C (160°C fan), Gas 4 and **line** two baking sheets with baking paper or use silicone baking sheets.

7. You will need to bake these biscuits in batches of no more than two on each sheet, as once they are cooked you will need to work quickly to **shape** them. When you get the hang of shaping them and into a rhythm you'll be able to have two trays in the oven while you are shaping a batch of biscuits.

8. Scoop the chocolate batter into a disposable piping bag and snip the end into a very fine point. Lay your template over one half of the baking paper or silicone baking mat, spoon 1 scant level tablespoon of plain batter

into the middle of the template and use an offset palette knife to quickly spread into a thin, even layer. Lift off the template and repeat on the other side of the baking paper or silicone mat.

9. Now take your disposable piping bag and **pipe** fine diagonal lines of the chocolate batter across each rectangle, keeping the chocolate lines neat and within the edges of the rectangle. Bake on the middle shelf of the oven for about 3–4 minutes, until just starting to brown at the edges.

10. Working quickly, remove the tray from the oven and slide a palette knife underneath each biscuit to loosen them from the paper. Flip the biscuits over and lay a drinking straw along one of the longer edges. Roll the biscuit into a tight spiral around the straw and place on a clean sheet of baking paper, seam side down. Repeat with the second biscuit. Leave these to cool for 2–3 minutes and then carefully pull the straw out of the spiral.

*Continued*

11. Continue to spread, pipe, bake and roll the biscuits until all of the mixture has been used up. You will need a clean sheet of baking paper each time you bake as it tends to ruckle and crease, making it hard to spread the batter thinly and evenly.

12. Once you have used up all of the batter and the cigarettes are neatly lined up, seam side down, on the lined baking tray, return them to the oven for 1–2 minutes to crisp up further. Leave until cold.

13. Prepare the ganache. Finely chop the 100g chocolate and tip into a bowl. Heat the 100ml cream with the 1 tablespoon of muscovado sugar, drop of vanilla extract and a pinch of salt in a small pan until the sugar has dissolved and the mixture just comes to the boil. Immediately remove from the heat, leave for 30 seconds and then pour over the chopped chocolate. Allow the chocolate to melt in the heat of the cream and then gently stir until smooth. Leave to cool and thicken slightly.

14 Spoon the cooled ganache into a disposable piping bag. Snip the end of the bag into a point and **pipe** the ganache into the middle of each cigarette. Leave until set.

15 **Melt** the 75g white and 75g dark chocolate for the decoration in separate heatproof bowls placed over a pan of barely simmering water (make sure the bottom of the bowl doesn't touch the water). Stir until smooth and leave to cool slightly. Mix together the 2 tablespoons of finely chopped hazelnuts and 2 tablespoons of finely chopped pistachios in a small bowl.

16 **Dip** one end of each filled cigarette into the melted white chocolate and the other end in the melted dark chocolate. Scatter with finely chopped nuts and leave on a clean sheet of baking paper until set.

# Chocolate and Vanilla Checkerboard Biscuits

These impressive-looking biscuits require a little precision and care, but once mastered they are easy enough and well worth the effort they take in time and concentration!

HANDS-ON TIME:
2 hours

BAKING TIME:
12–13 minutes

MAKES:
about 30 biscuits

SPECIAL
EQUIPMENT:
3–4 baking sheets,
ruler or tape measure,
20cm square cake
tin (optional),
pizza wheel
(optional),
palette knife

METHOD USED:
Creamed method,
page 25

*For the vanilla dough*

125g unsalted butter, at room temperature
75g caster sugar
50g icing sugar
1 teaspoon vanilla extract
1 large egg yolk
200g plain flour, plus extra for rolling out
50g ground almonds (or hazelnuts)
½ teaspoon baking powder
pinch of salt
1 tablespoon milk, plus extra for brushing

*For the chocolate dough*

125g unsalted butter, at room temperature
75g caster sugar
50g icing sugar
1 teaspoon vanilla extract
1 large egg yolk
175g plain flour
25g cocoa powder
50g ground almonds (or hazelnuts)
½ teaspoon baking powder
pinch of salt
1 tablespoon milk

1. Start by preparing the vanilla dough. Cream the butter with the caster sugar and icing sugar until pale and light. This is easiest and quickest using a free-standing mixer fitted with the creamer/paddle attachment. Scrape down the sides of the bowl, add the vanilla extract and mix again. Add the egg yolk and beat until combined.

2. Tip the flour, ground almonds, baking powder and salt into the bowl, add the milk and mix again until combined. Do not overmix the dough as it could become tough rather than crisp and

light. Gather the dough into a ball, flatten into a neat rectangle, cover with clingfilm and pop into the fridge.

3. Prepare the chocolate dough in the same way, adding the cocoa powder with the flour. Chill both the vanilla and chocolate dough for about 2 hours.

4. Divide both the vanilla and the chocolate dough in half as you'll find it easier to work with a smaller amount of dough. Lightly dust the work surface with plain flour and roll one half of the vanilla dough out into a square,

*Continued*

no more than 2mm thick and about 22cm square.

5. Lay the cake tin on top to use as a guide and, using a long kitchen knife or a pizza wheel, cut out a neat 20cm square. Carefully lift up the square, trying not to stretch it out of shape and place on a sheet of baking paper. Gather the off-cuts into a ball and set aside.

6. Roll one of the chocolate dough halves out in the same way and cut out another 20cm square. Gather the scraps into a ball and set aside. Lightly brush the vanilla square with a little milk and place the chocolate square neatly on top.

7. Using a ruler or tape measure mark the square into five strips, each 4cm wide. Using the knife (or a pizza wheel) cut the square into the five strips. Brush the top of the strip on the right with a little milk and lay the adjacent one on top of it so that it is now four alternate layers of dough.

8. Brush this one with milk and repeat this layering until you have stacked all the strips one on top of each other in alternately coloured layers. Carefully wrap this square log in baking paper and pop into the freezer while you prepare the remaining portions of vanilla and chocolate dough in the same way. Freeze both logs for 15–20 minutes.

9. Unwrap the first log and lay it so that the slices are stacked horizontally. Measure the width of the log and carefully mark it into four even-sized strips down the length – they should each be roughly 1cm wide and 20cm long. Starting on the right-hand side, cut the log into a slice using the marks as a guide. Lay this slice down flat on the parchment and lightly brush the top with milk. Cut the second slice and lay it on a palette knife. Turn this slice around by 180 degrees so that the layers are now the reverse of the first slice and lay the second slice on top of the first.

10. Repeat this slicing and layering, turning the alternate slices so the stack becomes a grid of alternate colours. Wrap in baking paper and freeze again for 20 minutes while you slice and layer the second log.

11. Finally, roll the vanilla dough off-cuts out into a rectangle roughly 17 × 20cm and trim one of the longer sides. Brush with milk and lay one of the square logs on top of the dough with the straight edges lined up. Roll the log neatly in vanilla dough as if you were wrapping a Battenberg cake in marzipan. Trim the end to neaten, wrap in baking paper and freeze for 40 minutes. Roll out the reserved chocolate dough in the same way and use to wrap the second log. Trim to neaten, wrap in baking paper and freeze as before.

12. Preheat the oven to 170°C (150°C fan), Gas 3 and **line** 3–4 baking sheets with baking paper.

13. Unwrap the first log from the baking paper, trim the ends and cut into slices no more than 2–3mm thick. Arrange on the prepared baking sheet, leaving a little space between each one to allow for spreading during cooking. Bake in batches on the middle shelf of the oven for about 12–13 minutes until firm and very pale golden at the edges. Repeat this slicing and baking with the second log. The biscuits will firm and crisp up further on cooling.

*Try Something Different*

**Sandwich** the biscuits together with a little chocolate hazelnut spread.

Gingerbread houses are fun to make but do require concentration and a little time to get them just right. Pop a night light candle inside as a festive touch to illuminate the stained glass.

## Up for a challenge

### For the dough

4 tablespoons golden syrup
2 tablespoons treacle
4 large egg yolks
600g plain flour, plus extra for rolling out
4 teaspoons ground ginger
2 teaspoons ground cinnamon
I teaspoon mixed spice
I ½ teaspoons baking powder
large pinch of salt
300g unsalted butter, chilled and diced
150g light muscovado sugar
75g caster sugar

### For the decoration

fruit-flavoured boiled sweets in assorted colours
500g royal icing sugar
sweets, candies and cake decorations

**HANDS-ON TIME:**
3+ hours,
plus setting

**BAKING TIME:**
12 minutes for
each panel but
1 hour in total

**MAKES:**
1 house

**SPECIALIST EQUIPMENT:**
several baking sheets,
assorted cutters
(rounds, squares,
hearts),
disposable
piping bags

**METHOD USED:**
Rubbed-in method,
page 22

1. Heat a measuring tablespoon up in a mug of boiling water for I minute – this makes it easy and less messy to measure the golden syrup and treacle. Spoon the golden syrup and treacle into a small bowl, add the egg yolks and mix well to combine.

2. Tip the flour, ginger, cinnamon, mixed spice, baking powder and salt into a large mixing bowl or into the bowl of a free-standing mixer. Add the chilled, diced butter and either **rub** in using your fingertips or by using the creamer/paddle attachment for the mixer. When there are no visible flecks of butter remaining add the light muscovado sugar and caster sugar and mix again to combine.

3. Make a well in the middle of the mixture, add the golden syrup, treacle and egg yolks and mix until the dough starts to come together into clumps. Using your hands, gently knead the dough until smooth but try not to over-work the dough or you will stretch the gluten strands in the flour, resulting in dough that is tough and may shrink and become misshapen during baking. Flatten the dough into a disc, weigh it and divide it in half – you should have two even pieces each weighing just over 700g. Wrap in clingfilm and chill for 2 hours.

4. Meanwhile photocopy the templates for the gingerbread house on page 162 and scale them up by 155 per cent so that they are the correct size; then cut them out.
*Continued*

5. Unwrap the boiled sweets and divide them into freezer bags so that each bag has just one colour. Double bag them (this will stop them spilling out of the bags) and using either a rolling pin, pestle or the bottom of a pan, lightly bash the sweets to break them up.

6. **Line** three solid baking sheets with baking paper and lightly dust the work surface with flour. Preheat the oven to 170°C (150°C fan), Gas 3.

7. Take one piece of the gingerbread dough and divide it into three portions – one of these portions should be slightly smaller than the other two. Roll out the smaller piece into a neat rectangle just slightly larger than the template for the house side walls. Lay the template on top and using a long, sharp knife or pizza cutter cut out the wall shape. Gather the off-cuts together and put to one side. Carefully lift the wall, trying not to stretch the dough out of shape, and place on a lined baking sheet. Using the cutters stamp out 2–4 window shapes from the wall and fill in the holes with crushed boiled sweets. Do not overfill the holes or the sweets will spill out over the edges of the window shapes as they melt. Chill for 15 minutes while you prepare the next sections.

8. Roll out one of the larger pieces of dough into a large, neat rectangle, this time slightly larger than the roof template. Lay the template on top and cut around it; reserve any off-cuts. Carefully lift onto a lined baking sheet and using one corner of a square biscuit-cutter stamp out small triangles from the bottom edge of the roof to make a fancy roof tile edge. Chill for 15 minutes.

9. Meanwhile roll the third piece of dough out as before and cut out the end wall, using the template as a guide. Using the knife cut out a door shape and place the door on the baking sheet. Use the cutters to stamp out windows in assorted shapes such as rounds, squares or hearts, fill the windows with crushed boiled sweets and chill as before.

10. Gather the off-cuts together, re-roll and cut out the four chimney sections, using the templates as a guide. If you like you can use any leftover dough to make gingerbread people to complete the scene.

11. Bake the gingerbread sections in batches on the middle shelf of the oven for 10–12 minutes, until firm and slightly darkened at the edges and the sweets have melted. It will still appear soft at this stage but will harden further on cooling. Leave to cool completely on the baking sheets.

12. Repeat with the second half of the dough – you should have two roof sections, two side walls, two end walls, four chimney pieces and one door – plus any optional gingerbread people.

13. Now comes the fun part: decorating and assembling. Choose the board or tray that you plan to display the gingerbread house on, as it will be almost impossible to move it once assembled.
*Continued*

157

14. Tip the 500g royal icing sugar into a bowl and gradually add water one tablespoon at a time, beating constantly until the icing is smooth and thick enough to hold a firm ribbon trail. Spoon half of the icing into a disposable **piping** bag (cover the remaining icing with clingfilm) and snip the end into a fine point. Pipe fine lines and dots around the window frames on each wall panel and pipe latticed windowpanes on the stained glass. Stick sweets, candies and cake decorations over the walls, using the royal icing as 'glue'. Be as creative as you like, perhaps enlisting the help of children. Pipe roof tiles over both roof sections and bricks over the chimney pieces. Leave the icing to dry for at least 30 minutes and for up to 1 hour.

15. Take one of the end walls and pipe a line of icing along the bottom edge. Stand this at one end of your board or tray with the best side facing outwards. Hold it in place for 2 minutes to allow the icing to start to set. You can also balance it against a glass for extra stability. Next pipe a line of icing along the bottom and side edges of a side wall section and press this at a right angle up against the end wall. Pipe an extra line of icing inside the join to act as extra 'cement', hold in place and stabilise with a glass on either side. Leave for 10 minutes until firm.

16. Repeat this process of piping and sticking with the remaining two wall sections, remembering to pipe inside the joins for stability. Once you have all

four walls upright leave them to dry and firm up for 1 hour. At this point you can also decorate the outside corners of the house with sweets sticking them on with icing – this not only looks pretty but also hides any untidy joins.

17. Meanwhile assemble the chimney. Take one rectangular section and lay it best-side down on the work surface. Pipe a line of icing along one of the long sides. Pipe icing along one long side of a cut-out chimney section and hold it vertically onto the first section (best side facing outwards) until secure. Repeat with the other cut-out section on the opposite side and finally secure a rectangular piece on top – you should now have a square chimney. Leave until set firm.

18. To secure the roof panels, pipe a line of icing along the upright and sloping roof lines on one side of the house and hold a roof panel in place, so that the top edge lines up with the top of the roof. (You may need a second pair of hands here.) Pipe extra 'cement' underneath the gable ends to secure and prop the bottom of the roof up with a jam jar or mug to hold it in place. Repeat with the second roof panel. Finally pipe a line of icing along the top of the roof and leave to set firm for 30 minutes before attaching the chimney.

19. Stand back and hold your breath.

# What biscuits shall I bake today?

# Conversion Tables

| WEIGHT | | | VOLUME | | | LINEAR | |
|---|---|---|---|---|---|---|---|
| **Metric** | **Imperial** | | **Metric** | **Imperial** | | **Metric** | **Imperial** |
| 25g | 1oz | | 30ml | 1fl oz | | 2.5cm | 1in |
| 50g | 2oz | | 50ml | 2fl oz | | 3cm | 1¼in |
| 75g | 2½oz | | 75ml | 3fl oz | | 4cm | 1½in |
| 85g | 3oz | | 125ml | 4fl oz | | 5cm | 2in |
| 100g | 4oz | | 150ml | ¼ pint | | 5.5cm | 2¼in |
| 125g | 4½oz | | 175ml | 6fl oz | | 6cm | 2½in |
| 140g | 5oz | | 200ml | 7fl oz | | 7cm | 2¾in |
| 175g | 6oz | | 225ml | 8fl oz | | 7.5cm | 3in |
| 200g | 7oz | | 300ml | ½ pint | | 8cm | 3¼in |
| 225g | 8oz | | 350ml | 12fl oz | | 9cm | 3½in |
| 250g | 9oz | | 400ml | 14fl oz | | 9.5cm | 3¾in |
| 280g | 10oz | | 450ml | ¾ pint | | 10cm | 4in |
| 300g | 11oz | | 500ml | 18fl oz | | 11cm | 4¼in |
| 350g | 12oz | | 600ml | 1 pint | | 12cm | 4½in |
| 375g | 13oz | | 725ml | 1¼ pints | | 13cm | 5in |
| 400g | 14oz | | 1 litre | 1¾ pints | | 14cm | 5½in |
| 425g | 15oz | | | | | 15cm | 6in |
| 450g | 1lb | | **SPOON MEASURES** | | | 16cm | 6½in |
| 500g | 1lb 2oz | | **Metric** | **Imperial** | | 17cm | 6½in |
| 550g | 1lb 4oz | | 5ml | 1 teaspoon | | 18cm | 7in |
| 600g | 1lb 5oz | | 10ml | 2 teaspoons | | 19cm | 7½in |
| 650g | 1lb 7oz | | 15ml | 1 tablespoon | | 20cm | 8in |
| 700g | 1lb 9oz | | 30ml | 2 tablespoons | | 22cm | 8½in |
| 750g | 1lb 10oz | | 45ml | 3 tablespoons | | 23cm | 9in |
| 800g | 1lb 12oz | | 60ml | 4 tablespoons | | 24cm | 9½in |
| 850g | 1lb 14oz | | 75ml | 5 tablespoons | | 25cm | 10in |
| 900g | 2lb | | | | | | |
| 950g | 2lb 2oz | | | | | | |
| 1kg | 2lb 4oz | | | | | | |

# Templates

Gingerbread House  (*see pages 154–159*)

Front and back wall
(x2)

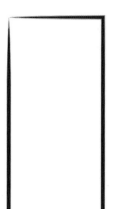 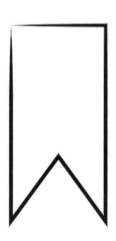

*Chimney: sides and back/front (x2 of each)*

*Side wall (x2)*

*Continued*

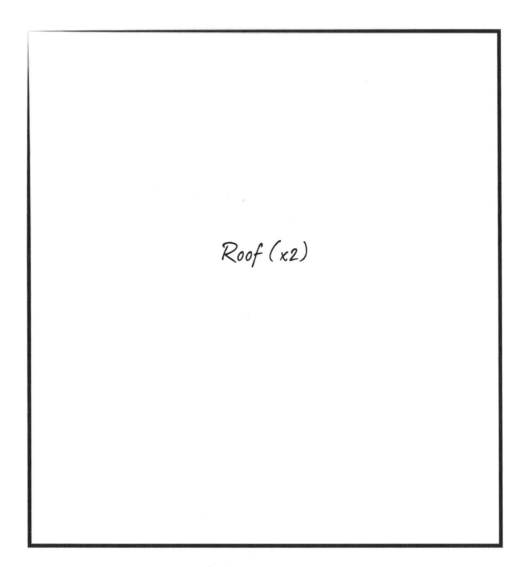

Roof (x2)

# *Index*

# Acknowledgements

Hodder & Stoughton and Love Productions would like to thank the following people for their contribution to this book:

Annie Rigg, Linda Collister, Laura Herring, Caroline McArthur, Sam Binnie, Helena Caldon, Alasdair Oliver, Kate Brunt, Laura Del Vescovo, Joanna Seaton, Sarah Christie, Anna Heath, Damian Horner, Auriol Bishop, Anna Beattie, Rupert Frisby, Jane Treasure, Sharon Powers.

First published in Great Britain in 2015
by Hodder & Stoughton
An Hachette UK company

1

Copyright © Love Productions Limited 2015

Design and Photography Copyright © Hodder & Stoughton 2015

A CIP catalogue record for this title is available from the British Library

Hardback ISBN 978 1 473 615274
Ebook ISBN  978 1 473 615281

Editorial Director: Nicky Ross
Editor: Sarah Hammond
Project Editor: Laura Herring
Series Editor: Linda Collister
Art Director: James Edgar
Layouts: Andrew Barker
Photographer: Amanda Heywood
Food Stylist: Joanna Farrow
Props Stylist: Linda Berlin

Typeset in Dear Joe, Mostra and Kings Caslon

Printed and bound in Italy by L.E.G.O. Spa

Hodder & Stoughton Ltd
Carmelite House
50 Victoria Embankment
London EC4Y 0DZ

www.hodder.co.uk

Continue on your journey to star baker with the other titles in *The Great British Bake Off: Bake It Better* series, the 'go to' baking books which give you all the recipes and baking know-how you'll ever need.

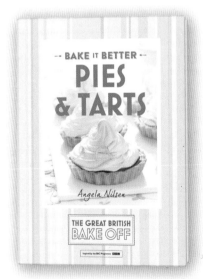

# DON'T JUST BAKE. BAKE IT BETTER.